# peter pan

This script is published by
DCG Publications.

All inquiries regarding purchase of further scripts and current royalty rates should be addressed to:

DCG Media Group
Vamos 73008
Chania
Crete
Greece

Email: info@dcgmediagroup.com
www.dcgmediagroup.com

Conditions

- All DCG Publication scripts are fully protected by the copyright acts. Under no circumstances must they be reproduced by photo-copying or any other means, either in whole or in part.

- The license to perform referred to above only relates to live performances of this script. A separate license is required for video-taping or sound recording, which will be issued on receipt of the appropriate fee.

- The name of the author shall be clearly stated on all publicity, programs etc. The program credits shall state "Script provided by DCG Publications".

# Peter Pan
## a musical fantasy

Adapted from the play by
J.M. Barrie

### Book & Lyrics
By

## Glyn Jones

### Music
By

## Andy Davidson

DCG
Publications

First Published in Greece 2010

© Glyn Jones & Andy Davidson 1994

The author's moral rights have been asserted

DCG Publications
www.dcgmediagroup.com

ISBN 978-960-98418-2-5

Typeset by
DCG Publications

Printed in England by
Lightening Source.

First Produced
at the
# Playhouse Theatre,
Weston-Super-Mare
December / Jnauary 1994-95

Directed by
Glyn Jones

Music
Andy Davidson

Choreography  Set design
Tracy Collier  Christopher Beeching

Lighting
Lawrence Doyle

## Cast List

Mr Darling / Captain Hook
Mrs Darling / Crocodile
Lisa / Tiger Lily
Nana / Mermaid
Peter
Wendy
John
Michael

Lost boys:
Slightly, Tootles, Curly, Nibs, 1st Twin, 2nd Twin

Pirates / Indians:
Smee
Cecco / Chief, Jukes / Running Dog, Starkey / Cunning Fox
Noodler / Bald Eagle

# Scenes

## Act One

| | |
|---|---|
| Scene One: | The Darling nursery |
| Scene Two: | The rooftops of London. |
| Scene Three: | A clearing in the forest – Neverland. |
| Scene Four: | Another part of the forest. |
| Scene Five: | Marooner's rock – The mermaids' lagoon. |

## Act Two

| | |
|---|---|
| Scene One: | Another part of the forest. |
| Scene Two: | The home underground. |
| Scene Three: | Another part of the forest. |
| Scene Four: | The pirate ship. |
| Scene Five: | A London street – The Darling home. |
| Scene Six: | The nursery. |

# Musical Numbers

1) OVERTURE

<u>ACT ONE</u>

| | | |
|---|---|---|
| 2) | NEVER IN THE NURSERY | Mr Darling |
| 3) | LULLABY | Mrs Darling |
| 4) | MY SHADOW AND ME | Peter |
| 5) | SECOND TO THE RIGHT | Peter, Wendy, John, Michael |
| 6) | PIRATE SONG | Hook & Pirates |
| 7) | SOGGY GREEN CAKE | Hook & Smee |
| 8) | INDIAN WAR DANCE | |
| 9) | A HOUSE IS NOT A HOME | Lost Boys |
| 10) | FANCY CROCODILE | Crocodile & Crockettes |
| 11) | SAILOR, SAILOR | Mermaid |
| 12) | PIRATE SONG (REPRISE) | |
| 13) | THE FIGHT ON MAROONER'S ROCK | |

<u>ACT TWO</u>

| | | |
|---|---|---|
| 14) | ENTR'ACTE | |
| 15) | A WONDERFULL TIME | Wendy & Peter |
| 16) | FOREVER (IS A LONG LONG TIME) | Peter *(Lyrics Davidson-Jones)* |
| 17) | MAKE UM SONG, MAKE UM DANCE | Tiger Lily, Wendy, John |
| 18) | PIRATE SONG (REPRISE) | |
| 19) | THE DOG WITH A HEART OF GOLD | Smee, Nana |
| 20) | LULLABY (REPRISE) | Mrs Darling |
| 21) | A HOUSE IS NOT A HOME (REPRISE) | Lost Boys |
| 22) | FOREVER (REPRISE) | Wendy |

The Darling nursery

# ACT ONE.

## SCENE ONE.

*The Nursery. Three doors: to landing, to day nursery, to bathroom. Three beds, bedside cabinets with night lights, table, chest of drawers, fireplace. Gas mantle upstage of landing door. Double windows, open. Window seat. Nana's kennel.*

*Before the OVERTURE ends the CURTAIN rises. It is early evening. The gaslight is on low. For a moment the room is empty and then TINKERBELL enters through the window, her light darting about the room as she looks for Peter's shadow. She disappears into a jar on the mantelpiece just as the OVERTURE reaches a climax with PETER leaping through the window and into the room.*

PETER: Tink? Tink! Where are you?

*TINK emerges from the jar.*

PETER: Have you found it?

*The sound of TINK's BELLS.*

PETER: Well what have you been doing all this time?

*TINK'S BELLS sound loudly.*

PETER: Thank you very much. I will look for it myself and there's no need to use bad language.

*PETER heads for the chest of drawers but stops as he hears MICHAEL's voice.*

MICHAEL: *(off)* I won't go to bed! I won't I won't!

*PETER leaps out of the window and TINK returns to her jar as MICHAEL appears from the day nursery being pushed, still protesting, into the room by NANA.*

MICHAEL:    Two minutes more. It isn't six o'clock yet. One minute! I don't want a bath. No, Nana, please!

*MRS DARLING appears at the landing door and turns up the gas.*

MRS DARL:   Michael! Are you being disobedient?

MICHAEL:    Who needs a bath? Who needs a bath?

MRS DARL:   You do. Now run along with Nana, there's a good boy.

*MICHAEL and NANA head for the bathroom and MRS DARLING crosses towards the day nursery door but suddenly stops and turns to stare at the open window. After a moment she moves to it and looks out, closes the window just as MR DARLING barges into the room.*

MR DARL:    Mary! Mary! Oh, there you are.

MRS DARL:   What is it, George?

MR DARL:    What is it? It's this tie, that's what it is! It will not tie. Certainly not around my neck. Round the bed-post, oh yes, twenty times round the bed-post, but round my neck? Oh, dear, no.

*WENDY and JOHN enter through the day nursery door. They are both in night attire though JOHN, still wearing his spectacles is also, for some reason, wearing a top hat and carrying a rolled umbrella.*

JOHN:       A little less noise there if you please.

MR DARL:    *(Turning)* What? *(Looking his son up and down)* Are you just off to the office?

JOHN:       No.

MR DARL:    Well, I warn you, Mary, all of you, that if this tie does not go round my neck I don't go out to dinner

|  |  |
|---|---|
|  | to-night, and if we don't go out to dinner to-night I never go to the office again, and if I don't go to the office again, *(to MARY)* you and I starve, and you *(to the CHILDREN)* will be thrown into the streets. |
| MRS DARL: | Here, let me try, dear. |

*Watched anxiously by WENDY and JOHN she starts to tie the tie. There is a screech and a lot of barking from the bathroom.*

| MR DARL: | A little less noise there if you please. |
|---|---|
| MRS DARL: | Do hold still, dear. |
| MR DARL: | Into bed, you two. |
| WENDY & JOHN: | Oh, dad! |
| MR DARL: | *(Imitating them)* Oh, dad! *(Thundering)* To bed! |

*Reluctantly they make for their beds. MRS DARLING has tied the tie and steps back.*

| MRS DARL: | There, dearest. It's done. |
|---|---|

*NANA enters to fetch a towel warming in front of the fire. She collides with MR DARLING who leaps back and starts frantically brushing his trousers.*

| MR DARL: | Mary, it's too bad! Just look at this, covered in hairs. Clumsy clumsy! |
|---|---|

*NANA gets her towel and goes back to the bathroom, a drooping figure, as MRS DARLING collects a clothes brush from the dressing table.*

| MRS DARL: | Here, dear, let me brush you. |
|---|---|
| MR DARL: | I sometimes think, Mary, that it's a mistake to have a dog for a nurse. |
| MRS DARL: | Oh, no, George! Nana's a treasure. |

MR DARL:        No doubt. But I have an uneasy feeling at times that she looks upon the children as puppies.

MRS DARL:       Oh, I don't think so. And, George *(She pulls him out of earshot of the beds)* we must keep Nana. I think the children might be in danger.

MUSIC.

MR DARL:        Danger!

MRS DARL:       Shhh! When I came into this room tonight I saw a face at the window.

MR DARL:        Oh, Mary! What on earth are you talking about? Three floors up!

MRS DARL:       I did see it, George, the face of a little boy. And this isn't the first time I've seen him.

MR DARL:        Oho? *(Meaning, "Why didn't you tell me this before?")*

MRS DARL:       Last week, on Nana's night out, I was sitting drowsing by the fire when I felt a draught, as if the window were open. And there he was...in the room.

MR DARL:        In the room? Oho!

MRS DARL:       Just then Nana came back and at once sprang at him. The boy leapt for the window. She closed it quickly but was too late to catch him. And do you know what happened?

MR DARL:        *(Disbelievingly sarcastic)* Do tell.

MRS DARL:       The boy escaped but his shadow had no time to get out. Bang went the window and cut it clean off.

MR DARL:        *(Still disbelieving)* Oh, Mary, Mary, so why didn't you keep this shadow?

MRS DARL: I did. I rolled it up and put it in the top drawer there.

JOHN: *(Who has been reading in bed, looks up from his book)* A little less noise there if you please.

WENDY: Yes, why are you two whispering? It's rude to whisper in public and you're going to be awfully late for your party.

*As the tete-a-tete breaks up NANA, with a bottle in her mouth and MICHAEL, in pyjamas, on her back (or with his arms around her neck) returns from the bathroom. He jumps from her back onto his bed and she heads for the table.*

MRS DARL: *(To WENDY)* It's all right, dearest. As soon as you're all safely tucked up we'll be on our way.

WENDY: Were you whispering secrets?

MRS DARL: Grown up talk, that's all, nothing to worry your pretty head about. What's that you've got there, Nana? Oh, of course; Michael, it's your medicine.

MICHAEL: Ugh! Won't take it.

MR DARL: Be a man, Michael. Be a man.

MICHAEL: Don't want to be a man.

MRS DARL: I'll get you a delicious chocky to take after it.

*She goes out.*

MR DARL: Don't pamper him, Mary. When I was your age, Michael, I took my medicine without a murmur. I still do.

WENDY: And your medicine's much nastier than Michael's, isn't it, father?

MR DARL: Much nastier. And, as an example to you, Michael, I

|          |                                                                                                 |
|----------|-------------------------------------------------------------------------------------------------|
|          | would take it now if I hadn't lost the bottle.                                                  |
| WENDY:   | *(Leaping out of bed and heading for the day nursery)* Oh, I know where it is!                  |
| MR DARL: | Wait!                                                                                           |

*But she has gone before he can stop her, especially as he bumps into NANA who lets out a howl of anguish and hops about nursing her trodden paw. He turns to JOHN for support.*

| MR DARL: | John, its disgusting stuff. It's that sweet sticky kind. |
|----------|-----------------------------------------------------------|
| JOHN:    | I'm sure you'll take it like a man, father.               |
| MR DARL: | Oh, thank you, thank you very much.                       |

*WENDY returns with a bottle and glass which she takes over to the table and starts to pour the medicine. MICHAEL is standing by the table. JOHN joins them and pours MICHAEL's medicine into a spoon.*

| WENDY:    | Now, Michael, you'll see how daddy takes his medicine. |
|-----------|--------------------------------------------------------|
| MR DARL:  | Michael first.                                         |
| MICHAEL:  | *(Shaking his head)* You first.                        |
| MR DARL:  | It will make me sick you know and I'm supposed to be taking your mother to a party. |
| JOHN:     | Come on, father.                                       |
| MR DARL:  | Don't you "come on father" me, young man.              |
| MICHAEL:  | I'm waiting.                                           |
| MR DARL:  | What for?                                              |
| MICHAEL:  | For you to take your medicine of course.               |

WENDY: Why don't you both take it at the same time?

MR DARL: Splendid idea. Are you ready, Michael?

*They both stand, spoon and glass suspended. Nothing happens.*

WENDY: All right then. On the count of three; one, two, three.

*MICHAEL takes his but MR DARLING whips his own glass behind his back. NANA shakes her head admonishingly and then, nose in air, returns to the bathroom.*

JOHN: Father, you cheated!

*MICHAEL starts to howl.*

MR DARL: I didn't! I meant to take it. Michael, stop that infernal row! I just sort of ... missed my mouth.

*The children all slope off to bed, MICHAEL still snivelling.*

MR DARL: Well it could easily happen couldn't it? I mean, look at the mess Michael always makes at mealtimes because he keeps missing his mouth. Hey! I've just thought of a splendid joke. Shhh!

*He pours his medicine into Nana's bowl.*

MR DARL: Don't say a word. She'll think its milk. *(Calling)* Nana! Nana!

WENDY: Daddy, no!

JOHN & MICHAEL: No no!

*MRS DARLING returns with the chocolate.*

MRS DARL: Daddy no, what?

MR DARL: Nothing, dear.

MRS DARL: Well, is it all over?

MR DARL:     All over, dear, quite satisfactorily. Ah, there you are, Nana. *(She has appeared from the bathroom)* Good dog, good girl, here's some milk for you.

MRS DARL:    And here's some chocolate for a good boy.

*She goes over to MICHAEL's bed as MR DARLING offers NANA the bowl. NANA crosses to drink. She sniffs the bowl, hurriedly backs away and retreats to her kennel.*

MRS DARL:    Why, Nana, whatever's the matter? George?

MR DARL:     It's nothing, nothing.

MRS DARL:    *(Picks up the bowl and sniffs it)* George!

MR DARL:     It was only a joke. Fat use my trying to be funny in this house.

WENDY:       Nana is crying.

MR DARL:     Oh, coddle her, go on, make a fuss. Nobody makes a fuss of me. Oh, no, I'm only the breadwinner in this house, why should I be coddled?

             COWS LIVE IN BYRES,
             CROWS PERCH ON WIRES,
             BUT NEVER A DOG IN THE NURSERY.
             MONKEYS IN TREES,
             HIVES ARE FOR BEES,
             BUT NEVER A DOG IN THE NURSERY.

             THE EAGLE IN HIS EYRIE,
             FEELS A LITTLE LEERY,
             YOU'LL FIND SLUGS UNDERNEATH THE LEAVES,
             BATS THAT HANG FROM EAVES.

             BADGERS IN SETS,
             BIRDS HAVE THEIR NESTS,
             BUT NEVER A DOG IN THE NURSERY.
             HORSES IN STABLES,

>MARTENS IN GABLES,
>BUT NEVER A DOG IN THE NURSERY.
>
>DOVES IN COTES ALL COOING,
>FROGS IN PONDS A-WOOING,
>THE STAG IS MONARCH OF THE GLEN,
>THE FOX IS IN HIS DEN.
>
>MOLES LIVE IN HOLES,
>PENGUINS AT POLES,
>BUT NEVER A DOG IN THE NURSERY.
>GORILLAS IN MOUNTAINS,
>FLAMINGO'S IN FOUNTAINS,
>BUT NEVER A DOG IN THE
>NEVER A NEVER A NEVER A DOG IN THE
>NURSERY, MY DEARS...
>AND THAT'S THAT!
>
>Nana! Come here. I refuse to allow this dog to lord it in my nursery for one hour longer. *(NANA pleads with him)* In vain, in vain, the proper place for you is in the yard, and there you go to be tied up this instant.

*He is dragging NANA by her collar towards the door.*

MRS DARL: George, George! Remember what I told you.

MR DARL: Am I master in this house or is she?

*They have gone.*

WENDY: He's going to chain her up!

*There is the sound of NANA barking.*

JOHN: She's awfully unhappy.

WENDY: That's not Nana's unhappy bark. That's her bark when she smells danger.

MRS DARL: Danger? Are you sure?

WENDY: Oh, yes; quite sure.

*MRS DARLING hurries to the window and looks out.*

JOHN: Is anything there?

MRS DARL: No, darling. All quite quiet and still. But, oh, how I wish I weren't going out tonight.

MICHAEL: Can anything harm us, mother?

MRS DARL: No, precious. Not after the nightlights are lit. They are the eyes a mother leaves behind to guard her children.

MRS DARL: THE HOURS FLY BY,
THE DAY IS ENDED,
WAS IT FILLED WITH FLOWERS FOR YOU?
PERHAPS SOME SHOWERS,
BUT THAT IS SOON MENDED,
WHEN SLEEP COMES THERE'S A RAINBOW OF EVERY HUE.
SLUMBER SAFE NEATH THE PALE MOONBEAMS,
AT THE END OF THE RAINBOW FIND YOUR DREAMS.
STARLIGHT, STAR BRIGHT,
LET ALL TROUBLES CEASE,
GIVE ME THE WISH I WISH TO-NIGHT,
MAY ALL THE CHILDREN OF THIS WORLD SLEEP IN PEACE.

*She has lit the nightlights, smoothed the coverlets, kissed the children good-night, etc., and finally leaves the room after turning off the gas. The room is now fairly dark. A second or two before TINK flies out of her jar and to the window which she opens for PETER to bound into the room.*

*TINK flies over to the chest of drawers and hovers in front of the top drawer.*

PETER: In there is it? I would have thought that would have been the first place to look, you silly fairy.

*There are angry noises from TINK as PETER opens the drawer and takes out his shadow.*

PETER: Oh, shut up, Tink, do.

*TINK flies into the drawer and PETER slams it shut. Her noise abruptly stops.*

PETER: Thank you.

*He moves to the centre of the room, leans on the table and, lifting one foot, tries to attach the shadow. It falls off. He tries the other foot. No go. He runs into the bathroom.*

PETER: Soap! Soap! Where's the soap?

*And returns with a bar of soap, sits on the floor and tries again, using the soap. The shadow will not stick. He is furious, then dejected. The noise wakes WENDY who sits up in bed and regards him curiously.*

WENDY: Boy, why are you crying?

*PETER jumps up, goes to the bed and bows. WENDY returns the bow from the bed.*

PETER: What is your name?

WENDY: Wendy Moira Angela Darling. What's yours?

PETER: Peter Pan.

WENDY: Is that all?

PETER: Yes.

WENDY: Where do you live?

*PETER runs to the window and points to the sky.*

PETER: Second to the right and then straight on till morning.

WENDY: What a funny address.

PETER: No it isn't.

WENDY: I mean, is that what they put on your letters?

PETER: Don't get any letters.

WENDY: But your mother gets letters.

PETER: Don't have a mother.

WENDY: Oh, Peter!

*She leaps out of bed to put her arms around him but he nimbly evades her.*

PETER: You mustn't touch me.

WENDY: Why ever not?

PETER: No one must ever touch me.

WENDY: Why?

PETER: I don't know.

WENDY: No wonder you were crying.

PETER: I wasn't crying. But I can't get my shadow to stick on. *(He shows her the shadow).*

WENDY: How awful! Oh, you silly thing. Soap won't do it. It will have to be sewn on.

PETER: What's "sewn"?

WENDY: You're terribly ignorant.

PETER: I am not!

WENDY: I will sew it on for you. But we must have more light.

*(She has crossed to the door and turns up the gas, then goes to the table for her sewing kit.)* Sit down. I daresay it will hurt a little.

PETER: That's all right. I'm used to that sort of thing. And I never cry.

*They are both on the floor and WENDY sews the shadow to his heels.*

WENDY: *(Thimble on finger)* I never thought I'd ever be sewing anything quite like this.

PETER: Why, what do you usually sew?

WENDY: Oh... samplers... things like that.

PETER: Samples of what?

WENDY: *(Laughing)* Oh, you really are so ignorant!

PETER: I'm not! I'm not! I'm the cleverest boy alive. Look at me! Look at me! *(He dances with his shadow)* Oh, the cleverness of me!

PETER: ME AND MY SHADOW ON THE WALL,
WORKING HARD,
STANDING GUARD,
WE ARE AFRAID OF NO ONE,
AFRAID OF NOTHING AT ALL.

ME AND MY SHADOW ON THE WALL,
THOUGH I KNOW,
I'LL NEVER GROW,
WHILE I HAVE GOT HIM BY ME,
IT DOESN'T MATTER AT ALL.

HE KNOWS MY EVERY SECRET,
HE'S SUCH A PART OF ME,
ALWAYS AT MY SHOULDER,
WHY SHOULD WE DISAGREE?

THAT'S HOW WITH FRIENDS IT OUGHT TO BE,
SIDE BY SIDE,
ON YOU STRIDE,
MAKING OUR WAY TOGETHER,
TWO OF US WILD AND FREE.

LIFE IS AN ADVENTURE,
THAT NEEDS A FRIEND TO SHARE.
WHEN SOMEBODY'S WITH YOU
THERE'S NOTHING YOU WON'T DARE?

ME AND MY SHADOW ON THE WALL,
KEEPING GUARD,
BATTLE-SCARRED,
WE ARE AFRAID OF NO ONE,
AFRAID OF NOTHING THING AT ALL,

ME AND MY SHADOW,
ME AND MY SHADOW,
MY SHADOW AND ME. *(He crows).*

WENDY: Well! You conceited thing. I did nothing of course.

PETER: You did a little I suppose.

WENDY: A little! If that's all the appreciation I get I might as well retire.

*She jumps into bed and pulls the clothes over her head. PETER leaps onto the bed.*

PETER: Oh, Wendy, don't retire. I can't help crowing when I'm pleased with myself. Wendy? Wen-dy. One girl is worth more than twenty boys.

*The head reappears.*

WENDY: Do you really think so?

PETER: I certainly do.

WENDY: I think so too.

PETER: Though there are, of course, exceptional boys, of whom I am one.

*They sit together on the side of the bed.*

WENDY: Of course there are. I shall give you a kiss if you like.

PETER: Thank you. *(He holds out his hand).*

WENDY: Don't you know what a kiss is?

PETER: I shall know when you've given it to me.

*Not to hurt his feelings she gives him her thimble.*

PETER: Thank you. Now shall I give you a kiss?

WENDY: If you please.

*She prepares herself for the kiss and is quite shocked when he pulls an acorn button of his jerkin, or from a pocket, and hands it to her.*

WENDY: Thank you. I will wear it on this chain around my neck. Peter, how old are you?

PETER: I don't know. But quite young I think. I ran away the day I was born.

WENDY: Ran away! Why?

PETER: Because I heard father and mother talking about what I was going to be when I grew up. But I didn't want to grow up. I want always to be a little boy and have fun. So I ran away to Kensington Gardens and lived a long time with the fairies.

WENDY: You know fairies!

PETER: Yes. But they're nearly all dead now. You see, Wendy, when the first baby laughed for the first time, the laugh broke into a thousand pieces and they all went skipping about, and that was the beginning of fairies. And now when every new baby is born its first laugh becomes a fairy. So there ought to be a fairy for every boy and girl.

WENDY: Isn't there?

PETER: Oh, no. Children know so much more nowadays. Or, at least, they think they do. And every time a child says, "I don't believe in fairies" a fairy somewhere drops down dead. *(He skips about heartlessly; stops)* Which reminds me...where could she have gone to? Tinker Bell, Tink, where are you?

WENDY: Peter! You mean to say there's a fairy in this room?

PETER: Shhh! You don't hear anything do you?

WENDY: *(Nodding)* It sounds like bells, tiny bells.

PETER: I hear it too. That's fairy language.

WENDY: And it seems to be coming from over there.

PETER: *(Shrieking with laughter)* I do believe I shut her in that drawer.

*He releases TINK who darts about the room in an absolute fury.*

PETER: Oh, Wendy, it's just as well you don't understand fairy language; she's saying the most dreadful things.

WENDY: Ask her to keep still. I want to see her.

PETER: Oh, they never stay still, not for a moment. *(To TINK)* Well, I'm sorry, how was I to know you were in the drawer?

*A barrage from TINK.*

WENDY: What did she say?

PETER: She says you're a great ugly girl and I'm a silly ass. She's really quite common you know. Ignore her.

WENDY: Peter, when you take the second to the right and go straight on till morning where does it get you?

PETER: To the Never Land of course. Now who's ignorant? I live there with the lost boys. I'm their captain.

WENDY: What fun it must be.

PETER: Yes. But sometimes we do get a bit lonely. It wouldn't be so lonely if we had someone like you with us.

WENDY: Ouch!

PETER: What is it?

WENDY: It felt like someone was pulling my hair.

PETER: That was Tink. I've never known her so naughty before.

WENDY: Shhh. *(She turns down the gas)* Peter, why did you come to our nursery window?

PETER: To hear stories. None of us knows any stories. Your mother was telling you all about the prince who couldn't find the lady who wore the glass slipper.

WENDY: Cinderella. He did find her and they lived happily ever after.

PETER: I'm glad.

*He is up and heading for the window.*

WENDY: Where are you going?

PETER: To tell the others.

WENDY: Don't go, Peter. I know lots of stories.

PETER: Then come with me. We'll fly.

*TINK retires to the vase to sulk.*

WENDY: Fly? I can't fly.

PETER: I'll teach you. I'll teach you to jump on the back of the wind and then away we go. Wendy, when you're sleeping in your silly bed you could be flying about with me saying funny things to the stars. There are mermaids, Wendy, with long tails. And how we would all respect you.

WENDY: Would you teach John and Michael to fly too?

PETER: Oh, if you like.

WENDY: *(Shaking him)* John! John! Wake up! There's a boy here who's to teach us to fly.

JOHN: *(Still half-asleep)* What? What?

WENDY: Michael, open your eyes. We're going to learn to fly.

MICHAEL: To fly?

*All three gather around PETER but then NANA's bark is heard.*

JOHN: Quick, hide!

*They all hide in appropriate places to be hooked up.*

*The door opens and LIZA appears with a firm hand on NANA's chain.*

LIZA: There, you suspicious brute, all safe and sound aren't they? Every one of the little angels fast asleep in bed. So what's the matter with you?

*NANA growls.*

LIZA: Now no more of your nonsense, Nana. I warn you, if you bark again I shall go straight for master and missus and bring them home from the party, and then won't master just whallop you. Come along, you naughty dog.

*LIZA drags NANA out and closes the door. The children and PETER emerge from the hiding places.*

JOHN: Is it true, you can really fly?

PETER: Look.

*He swoops up.*

WENDY: *(Clapping her hands)* Oh, how sweet!

PETER: *(Crowing)* I'm sweet, oh, I'm so sweet.

JOHN: I say, a little less noise there if you please.

*They all put their fingers to their lips then, as PETER floats overhead, they all make unsuccessful attempts to fly.*

JOHN: How do you do it?

PETER You just think lovely, wonderful thoughts and they lift you up in the air.

JOHN: I can't get off the ground!

MICHAEL: Me can't neither.

PETER: I must blow the fairy dust on you. *(He wipes his hands on his jerkin and shakes the dust on them.)* Now try. Try from the bed. Just wriggle your shoulders this way and then let go.

*MICHAEL is the first to fly.*

MICHAEL: I flewed! I flewed! Look at me! Look at me!

| | |
|---|---|
| WENDY: | It's lovely! |
| JOHN: | Fantastic! |
| MICHAEL: | I like it! I like it! |
| JOHN: | Why don't we go out? |
| PETER: | There are pirates. |
| JOHN: | Pirates! *(He grabs his hat and umbrella)*. What are we waiting for? |

*One by one they fly out the window. TINK is the last to go. Reappearing from the vase she buzzes about and then disappears just as the door flies open and MR & MRS DARLING and a barking NANA appear. NANA dashes for the window. MR DARLING turns up the gas and they survey the empty room.*

MUSIC.

MRS DARL: Oh, my children... my children...

*MR and MRS DARLING comfort each other as the LIGHTS fade and SCENE CHANGES to*


SCENE TWO.

*The rooftops of London with PETER, WENDY, JOHN & MICHAEL flying off to Never Land.*

PETER:  SECOND TO THE RIGHT,
AND STRAIGHT ON TILL MORNING,
YOU'LL ARRIVE AT NEVER LAND,
JUST AS DAY IS DAWNING.
YOU DON'T NEED FEATHERS,
YOU DON'T NEED WINGS,
YOU JUST HAVE TO THINK OF WONDERFUL THINGS,
AND YOU'LL FLY,

|        | |
|---|---|
| | YOU WILL FLY, |
| | YOU'LL SWOOP TO THE GROUND, |
| | AND THEN WITH ONE BOUND, |
| | YOU'LL SOAR THROUGH THE SKY, |
| | AND NO MATTER HOW FAR, |
| | YOU'LL REACH YOUR FAVOURITE STAR. |
| ALL: | SECOND TO THE RIGHT, |
| | AND STRAIGHT ON TILL MORNING, |
| | WE'LL ARRIVE IN NEVER LAND, |
| | JUST AS DAY IS DAWNING, |
| | YOU DON'T NEED FEATHERS, |
| | YOU DON'T NEED WINGS, |
| | YOU JUST HAVE TO THINK OF WONDERFUL THINGS, |
| | AND YOU'LL FLY |
| | YOU WILL FLY |
| | AND ARRIVE IN NEVER LAND |
| | JUST AS DAY IS DAWNING, |
| | JUST AS DAY IS DAWNING, |
| | JUST AS DAY IS DAWNING. |

*Their voices fade away as they fly out.*

MUSIC.

### SCENE THREE.

*The clearing above the Lost Boys' home. Trees each with a "door" hole.*

*SLIGHTLY is seated on a mushroom or a rock playing his PIPES. He stops to look up at the sky and is about to play again when TOOTLES' head appears at his door.*

TOOTLES: Any sign of Peter yet?

SLIGHTLY: No, Tootles, no.

*CURLY appears, climbing out of his tree.*

CURLY: I do wish he'd come back.

TOOTLES: *(Climbing out, bringing with him his bow and arrows)* I'm always afraid of the pirates when Peter's not here.

SLIGHTLY: Huh! I'm never afraid of pirates. Nothing scares me. But I'd like to know more about Cinderella.

*He starts to play his PIPES again just as THE TWINS appear.*

1ST TWIN: I know what happened to Cinderella, Slightly.

SLIGHTLY: You do?

1ST TWIN: Yes, in the end the prince found her.

2ND TWIN: How do you know that?

1ST TWIN: I dreamt it last night.

*NIBS joins them.*

2nd TWIN: Well I don't think you should have dreamt it because I didn't and, being twins, we should have the same dream.

1ST TWIN: Sorry. I won't do it again.

TOOTLES: I think my mother must have been rather like Cinderella.

NIBS: Mine too.

SLIGHTLY: My mother was fonder of me than your mothers were of you.

*Uproar.*

SLIGHTLY: Oh, yes, she was. Peter had to make up names for all of you but my mother had wrote my name on the clothes I was lost in. "Slightly Soiled", that's my name.

MUSIC.

A clearing in the forest - Neverland

*More uproar until they hear the VOICES OFF.*

PIRATES: YO HO, YO HO, THE PIRATE LIFE,
THE FLAG OF SKULL AND BONES,
A MERRY HOUR, A HEMPEN ROPE,
AND HEY FOR DAVY JONES.

*By the end of the verse all the BOYS have disappeared down their various boltholes, with the exception of NIBS who panics and, after running around in circles, disappears behind the trees.*

*The PIRATES enter dancing.*

*CAPTAIN HOOK, his hand resting on a chest marked "Treasure", is borne on in a palanquin decorated with the skull and crossbones and carried by CECCO, BILL JUKES, GENTLEMAN STARKEY and NOODLER with SMEE following up behind.*

*SMEE, who is not paying much attention, doesn't realise they have stopped and put down the palanquin with the result that he topples over onto HOOK displacing his hat and wig. HOOK, furious, leaps roaring to his feet, straightens his headgear and menaces SMEE with his hook. SMEE loses his glasses.*

HOOK: Smee! You lolloping landlubber, what do you think you're at?

SMEE: N-n-nothing, captain.

HOOK: Dost want a taste of my hook?

SMEE: N-n-n-no thank you, captain.

*Fortunately for SMEE, HOOK is distracted by the sight of STARKEY raising his pistol as NIBS darts from behind a tree and disappears again. The hook is immediately twisted in STARKEY's arm. SMEE meanwhile is on hands and knees searching for his glasses.*

STARKEY: Captain, let go!

HOOK: Put up your pistol first.

STARKEY: Twas one of those boys you hate. I could have shot him dead.

HOOK: Aye, and the sound would have brought Tiger Lily's redskins on us. Do you want to lose your scalp?

NOODLER: *(Drawing his cutlass)* Shall I after him, captain, and tickle him with Johnny Corkscrew? Johnny is a silent fellow.

*He feels the edge of the blade and faints as he draws his own blood. He is caught by CECCO and JUKES.*

HOOK: Not now. He is only one, and I want to horribly mischief all seven of them. Scatter and seek them out.

*With "Aye-aye Captain" and JUKES blowing his bosun's whistle they go their separate ways. HOOK sits on a surprised SMEE'S back.*

HOOK: Most of all I want their captain, Peter Pan. Twas he cut off my arm. Oh, I have waited long to shake his hand with this. Oh, I'll tear him!

*He slashes down with the hook which whistles past SMEE'S nose. SMEE, who has found and put on his glasses, screams. HOOK shrieks and leaps to his feet, turning to see SMEE still on all fours.*

HOOK: Cod's roe and shark's teeth, Smee! What in the name of Neptune are you up to now? You almost caused me a heart-attack.

SMEE: S-s-s-sorry, captain. I was looking for my glasses.

HOOK: Surely you are aware that I am of the most delicate constitution. Except for this. *(Brandishing his hook in front of SMEE's nose and rising to a crescendo).* Of course!

SMEE: Indeed, captain, very true, captain. *(He delicately*

|        | *pushes the hook out of striking distance)* And yet I have often heard you say your hook is worth a score of hands, for dressing the wig, picking the teeth, and other such homely uses. |
|--------|---|
| HOOK:  | *(Mollified)* Ah, yes... how right you are, Smee. Tis a useful instrument indeed, don't think I am not aware of that. An octopus with eight arms is not more versatile. I should thank Peter Pan for the favour except for one thing. |
| SMEE:  | Don't captain, don't! |

*SMEE covers his ears. HOOK unhooks one hand and removes the other.*

| HOOK:  | You shall hear, Smee, you shall hear. |
|--------|---|
| SMEE:  | *(As fast as he can)* Pan flung your arm to a crocodile that happened to be passing by and the brute found it so tasty it's followed you ever since, from sea to sea, from land to land, licking its lips for the rest of you. *(Then placatingly)* Look on it this way, captain, it's a sort of a compliment really. |
| HOOK:  | I want no such compliments! *(He sits on a toadstool)* I want Peter Pan who first gave the brute its taste for me. Smee, that crocodile would have had me before now but by a lucky chance... |
| SMEE:  | It swallowed a clock and it goes tick tick tick inside and, so before ... |
| HOOK:  | It can reach me I hear the tick and bolt. Exactly so. |
| SMEE:  | Someday the clock will run down and then it will get you. |

*HOOK gives a little shriek and bites his nails.*

| SMEE:  | *(Removing HOOK's fingers from his mouth)* There, there, captain. Don't take on so. |
|--------|---|

HOOK: But that is the fear that haunts me, Smee. Sharkfins and whale blubber! This seat is hot! I am burning.

*He hastily rises, rubbing his backside, and the two of them examine the mushroom on which he was sitting. HOOK lifts the mushroom to reveal a chimney from which there appears a wisp of smoke, also the sound of children's voices.*

SMEE: A chimbley!

HOOK: *(Replaces the mushroom)* So this is their hideout, underground. We've got them, Smee.

SMEE: We have?

HOOK: Smee, what would any small boy simply die for?

SMEE: A bottle of rum?

*SMEE gets a playful slap on the cheek, not with the hook.*

HOOK: Think again, Smee.

SMEE: A bike?

*Another playful slap.*

HOOK: Again.

SMEE: Er...a lady companion.

*Another slap.*

SMEE: *(Quickly)* A mother!

*The hand is raised but stops halfway and HOOK puts his arm around SMEE's shoulder.*

HOOK: Ye-es. But I think that applies to all of us does it not? You're obviously not trying, Smee. *(Taps him on the chest with the hook.)*

*SMEE's knees start to knock, his teeth to chatter.*

HOOK:     Cake, Smee. Cake.

SMEE:     Cake?

HOOK:     Cake.

> DEVIL'S FOOD CAKE AND ANGEL CAKE,
> CHOCOLATE ECLAIRS AND DOUGHNUTS,
> THEN NO MATTER WHAT ELSE IS AT STAKE,
> ANY SMALL BOY WILL GO NUTS FOR
> JUST THE PROMISE, JUST THE THOUGHT,
> OF APFEL STRUDEL AND LINDE TORTE.
>
> EYES LIGHTING UP FOR ALMOND FLAN,
> LICKING THEIR LIPS AND SIGHING,
> CUSTARD SLICES ARE NOT IN MY PLAN,
> SOON THEY WILL ALL BE DYING FOR
> JUST ONE SLICE OF WHAT I BAKE,
> A GIANT, FATALLY TEMPTING CAKE
>
> Green, I think.

SMEE:     Green?

HOOK:     Yes, green. What boy can resist green?

> THEY'LL COME UNSTUCK,
> THEY'LL COME UNGLUED,
> AND KNOWING MY LUCK,
> I'LL NEVER BE SUED,
> WHEN THEY DIE,
> WHEN THEY DIE,
> WHEN THEY DIE
> DIDDLY AY DI DEE DI DI DEE DI,
> AND I'LL BET A DUCKET,
> THEY'LL ALL KICK THE BUCKET,
> AND THAT'S HOW MY PLAN WILL CONCLUDE
> AND THAT'S HOW MY PLAN WILL CONCLUDE.

SMEE:     It's the wickedest, prettiest plan I ever did hear of.

| | |
|---|---|
| HOOK: | BATTENBERG CAKE WITH MARZIPAN, |
| SMEE: | STRAWBERRY TABATIERES, |
| HOOK: | SIMNEL, MARBLE AND DUNDEE WILL FAN FLAMES OF GREED IN LITTLE DEARS, BUT FOR SOMETHING REALLY MEAN, THERE'S NOTHING GROSSER THAN CAKE THAT'S GREEN. |
| SMEE: | What about a nice Plum-Guava Latticework Tart? |
| HOOK: | No no no no! TIRAMISU FOR ME AND YOU, |
| SMEE: | BUT THERE'S NOTHING A BOY LIKES BETTER, |
| HOOK: | THAN DAMPLY RICH, |
| SMEE: | RICHLY DAMP, |
| HOOK: | EVER SO TASTY, |
| SMEE: | NICER THAN PASTRY, |
| TOGETHER: | DELICIOUSLY SCRUMPTIOUS SPLENDIDLY SUMPTUOUS SOGGY GREEN CAKE. SOGGY GREEN CAKE. OI! |
| HOOK: | Come, Smee, we must put my plan into action. We will leave the cake on the shore of the mermaid's lagoon where they will find it and gobble it up. This way, I think. |

TOM TOMS.

*There are yells and whoops offstage*

| | |
|---|---|
| HOOK: | Cast anchor, Smee! Cast anchor! |
| SMEE: | This way, Cap'n. |

*They pick up the litter and scurry off in the opposite direction just as TIGER LILY, THE CHIEF, RUNNING DOG, CUNNING FOX & BALD EAGLE appear. They dance on and all put their ears to the ground then sit up.*

TIGER LILY: Pirates! Have um scalp. What you say?

BRAVES: Ugh.

TIGER LILY: Which way?

BRAVES: This way.

*They all point in different directions and dance off.*

*NIBS runs on.*

NIBS: *(Calling)* Tootles, Slightly, Twins!

*The BOYS appear.*

NIBS; They've all gone.

TOOTLES: Did you see the pirates?

NIBS: Yes. Indians too! But I saw a wonderfuller thing, Tootles. High over the lagoon I saw the loveliest great white bird and it's flying this way.

TOOTLES: What kind of a bird?

NIBS: I don't know. But it looked so weary and, as it flies, it moans, "Poor Wendy".

SLIGHTLY: I remember now, there are birds called Wendies.

1ST TWIN: Look! Here it comes, the Wendy.

2nd TWIN: Tinker Bell's with her.

TOOTLES: She's trying to hurt the Wendy! Hey, Tink!

NIBS: She says Peter wants us to shoot the Wendy.

SLIGHTLY: All right then, quick, bows and arrows!

TOOTLES: *(First with his bow)* Out of the way, Tink!

*He takes aim and shoots. WENDY flutters down, the arrow in her breast.*

TOOTLES: I've shot the Wendy! Peter will be pleased.

*There is a tinkle and what sounds suspiciously like fairy laughter from TINK settled in a tree.*

1ST TWIN: She called you a silly ass.

TOOTLES: *(To TINK)* Why did you say that?

*The BOYS, sensing TOOTLES might have blundered, draw away. SLIGHTLY kneels down to examine WENDY.*

SLIGHTLY: This isn't a bird. It's a lady.

NIBS: And Tootles has killed her.

CURLY: I think Peter was bringing her here to take care of us.

2nd TWIN: Yes, and Tootles has killed her.

CURLY: Poor Tootles. Peter's going to be ever so mad. That's all I can say. Glad it wasn't me killed the Wendy.

*There is a general murmur of agreement.*

TWINS: Poor Tootles.

SLIGHTLY: If I were you, Tootles I'd make myself scarce pretty quick.

*There is the sound of PETER crowing.*

SLIGHTLY: Too late.

*They form a group to hide WENDY as PETER swoops down.*

PETER: Greetings, men. I'm back. (Silence) Didn't you hear me? I said, I'm back. Why don't you cheer? Well come on. All right then, great news, boys, I have brought you a mother.

CURLY: We know.

1ST TWIN: Oh, mournful day.

2ND TWIN: Oh, woeful day.

TOOTLES: Peter, I will show her to you. Stand back and let Peter see.

*They do so*

PETER: Wendy! Dead? *(He kneels and plucks out the arrow).*

CURLY: I thought it was only flowers that die.

PETER: Whose arrow?

*They all turn to look at TOOTLES.*

PETER: Tootles!

*He raises the arrow as if to strike but somehow cannot do it. In fact, behind him, WENDY has raised her arm.*

NIBS: I think the Wendy bird, I mean, lady, said something.

SLIGHTLY: I heard it too. I think she said, "Poor Tootles".

PETER: *(Investigating)* She lives.

SLIGHTLY: The Wendy lady lives.

*They all nod and give themselves a round of applause.*

PETER: *(Holding up a button attached to the chain round Wendy's neck).* See? The arrow struck against this. It's a kiss I gave her. It saved her life.

SLIGHTLY: I remember kisses; let me see it. *(He takes it)* hmnn.... Yes, that's a kiss all right.

PETER: Wendy, get better quickly and I'll take you to see the mermaids. She's awfully anxious to see a mermaid.

*TINKER BELL, who disappeared the moment WENDY was shot, now reappears tinkling gaily, obviously under the impression her rival is no more.*

CURLY: Listen to Tink how happy she is. She thinks the Wendy is dead. Tink, the Wendy lady lives.

*TINK is furious.*

1ST TWIN: She told us...

TWINS: ...you wanted us to shoot the Wendy.

PETER: She what?

*They all solemnly nod.*

PETER: Then, listen, Tink, I am your friend no more.

*TINK responds, possibly meaning "who cares?"*

PETER: Go! I never want to see you again.

*Now it is more of a tearful tinkle.*

SLIGHTLY: She's crying.

TOOTLES: She says she's your fairy.

PETER: Oh, all right, not forever then, but for a whole week.

*TINK slopes off, sulking.*

PETER: Now, what shall we do with the Wendy?

TOOTLES: If she lies there she will die.

SLIGHTLY: Yes. It's a pity, I suppose she will. But there's no way out.

PETER: Yes there is. Let's build a house around her. Get to it.

*But, before the BOYS can disperse, JOHN and MICHAEL, bedraggled and tired, wander in.*

TOOTLES: Ho-ho!

TWINS: Ho-ho! Ho-Ho!

SLIGHTLY: Attack!

*They surge forward. MICHAEL shrieks and falls back and JOHN is prepared to defend them with his umbrella when PETER, dagger drawn, gets in between.*

PETER: Back! Back! Back, I say!

JOHN: It's true, we did fly. And here's Peter. Peter, is this the place?

PETER: Yes. Who are you?

JOHN: John.

MICHAEL: Michael.

JOHN: Where's Wendy?

MICHAEL: There she is. She's asleep. Wake her up, John. She can make us some supper. I'm hungry.

PETER: Curly, see that these boys help build the house.

JOHN: Build a house?

CURLY: For the Wendy.

*The BOYS all set about building the Wendy House, going off and bringing on the materials, with a song and a dance putting up the house around the prostrate WENDY.*

| | |
|---|---|
| JOHN: | A HOUSE HAS A FLOOR, |
| | AND A NEAT FRONT DOOR, |
| | FOUR WALLS OR MORE, |
| | AND A WATERPROOF ROOF. |
| | |
| | A CAT BY THE HEARTH, |
| | AND A GARDEN PATH, |
| | EVEN A BATH, |
| | FOR A RUB A DUB-DUB. |
| | |
| | BUT A HOUSE IS NOT A HOME WITHOUT A MOTHER, |
| ALL: | A HOUSE IS NOT A HOME WITHOUT A MUM, |
| | MORE THAN A SISTER OR A BROTHER, |
| | SHE'LL ALWAYS BE A BOY'S BEST CHUM. |
| | |
| JOHN: | A HOUSE IS A NEST, |
| TOOTLES: | THE PLACE YOU LOVE BEST, |
| BOTH: | WHERE YOU CAN REST, |
| | AND DREAM YOUR DREAMS AWAY. |
| | |
| | A HOUSE WILL HAVE BEDS, |
| | WITH COMFORTABLE SPREADS, |
| | TO LAY YOUR HEADS, |
| | AT THE END OF THE DAY. |
| | |
| PETER: | BUT A HOUSE IS NOT A HOME WITHOUT A MOTHER, |
| | A HOUSE IS NOT A HOME WITHOUT A MUM. |
| | MORE THAN A SISTER OR A BROTHER, |
| | SHE'LL ALWAYS BE A BOY'S BEST CHUM. |
| | |
| ALL: | NO A HOUSE IS NOT A HOME WITHOUT A MOTHER, |
| | A HOUSE IS NOT A HOME WITHOUT A MUM. |
| | MORE THAN A SISTER OR A BROTHER, |
| | SHE'LL ALWAYS BE A BOY'S BEST CHUM. |
| | MORE THAN A SISTER OR A BROTHER, |

SHE'LL ALWAYS BE A BOY'S BEST CHUM.

*They dance and the last line is repeated until the house is done.*

1ST TWIN: There, I think it's finished.

PETER: There's no knocker on the door.

*TOOTLES hangs up his shoe.*

PETER: There's no chimney.

JOHN: It certainly does need a chimney.

*PETER seizes JOHN's hat, knocks out the top and places it on the roof. A little curl of smoke rises up.*

PETER: Right, all look your best. First impressions are most important.

*He knocks. The door opens and WENDY appears. They all bow, JOHN and MICHAEL being kicked into it.*

SLIGHTLY: Wendy lady, for you we built this house.

NIBS: Are you pleased?

WENDY: Oh, yes. It's a wonderful house.

TWINS: And we are your children.

WENDY: Oh!

*They all kneel, JOHN and MICHAEL being pulled down.*

ALL: Wendy lady, be our mother.

WENDY: I don't know if I should. I don't really have any experience.

PETER: That doesn't matter. All we need is a nice motherly person.

Another part of the forest

WENDY: In that case, if you'll all come inside, I might just have time to finish the story of Cinderella before bedtime.

*And with a great deal of noise all, except PETER, enter the house. He draws his dagger and feints a few times at an imaginary foe.*

### SCENE FOUR.

*Another part of the forest.*

*An exhausted, dishevelled HOOK and SMEE stagger on. They stop to rest, sitting on the palanquin.*

HOOK: Do you think it's safe to stop, Smee?

SMEE: *(Panting heavily and mopping his brow)* I th-th-th-think so, Cap'n.

HOOK: You don't hear anything.

SMEE: *(After listening)* No, Cap'n. Yes Cap'n

HOOK: What? What?

SMEE: Indians. Cap'n. Caught up with us they have.

*And, sure enough, again we hear the whooping of Indian braves.*

HOOK: Quick, Smee! Hide! Hide!

*There is a moment of panic as they run in circles, bump into each other and then HOOK dives into the palanquin and SMEE runs off*

*HOOK pulls the curtains shut just as TIGER LILY leads on her BRAVES and stops them with an imperious lifting of the hand. They regard the palanquin with suspicion. TIGER LILY raises a finger to her lips and indicates for two of the BRAVES to part the curtains. They do so.*

*The palanquin is empty.*

*They go around the back and open those curtains. No sign of anybody. The other two kneel down and lift the fringe. Nothing. HOOK has completely disappeared.*

*Bewildered, they close the curtains.*

TIGER LILY: Go. Find'um pirates. Bring'um scalps.

*Whooping and hollering, the BRAVES depart leaving TIGER LILY standing in front of the palanquin and looking very suspicious.*

*The curtains suddenly open; she is grabbed by HOOK and bundled into the palanquin. SMEE returns. The curtains are drawn again and, after a moment, HOOK and SMEE emerge from the back. If HOOK had two hands he would be rubbing them with glee.*

HOOK: Odd socks and bare bodkins, Smee, what a prize! What a catch! What will we do with her?

SMEE: Make her walk the plank, Cap'n.

HOOK: No, no, no. Something more refined, Smee; slower, more torturous. I have it! Marooner's Rock! The tide will rise slowly, oh, so slowly. If I could control time it would rise even more slowly.

SMEE: Talking of time, Cap'n, do you hear something else?

HOOK: *(Panic)* What? What?

*They listen. There is the TICK TICK TICK of a clock.*

HOOK: *(Shrieking)* Away, Smee! Full sail ahead! Away! Away!

*They take up the palanquin and scurry off just as the CROCODILE enters.*

*This is no ordinary CROCODILE that slithers and slides. This is an upright voluptuous lady CROCODILE who will shimmy on like Mae West. She can carry her tail over her arm. She can be accompanied by a troupe of toe-tapping CROCODILES known as THE CROCKETTES.)*

CROC: I'M A FANCY CROCODILE,
WITH A HEAVENLY SMILE,
BUT WHEN HE SEES ME HE RUNS A MILE.
SO WHAT HAVE I DONE,
TO MAKE THAT MAN RUN?
WHEN ALL I WANT TO DO IS EAT HIM UP.

THOUGH MY HIDE IS ROUGH AND TOUGH,
AND MY MANNER SOMEWHAT BLUFF,
I'M FASCINATING AND CUTE ENOUGH
TO CATCH ANY MAN,
BELIEVE ME I CAN
THEN ALL I'LL WANT TO DO IS EAT HIM UP.

BARBECUED STEAKS
MAY HAVE WHAT IT TAKES,
BUT IF YOU CAN ACQUIRE IT,
CHECK THIS OUT,
YOU'LL JUST LOVE TO DIP YOUR SNOUT,
IN TENDER LOIN OF PIRATE.

I'M A CROCODILE WITH STYLE,
FULL OF FEMININE GUILE,
AND EVEN IF YOU BELIEVE I'M VILE
TO SCHEME AND PLOT,
FOR PIRATE HOT-POT,
I DON'T CARE,
SO THERE,
MY GASTRIC JUICE IS FLOWING,
AT THE CERTAINTY OF KNOWING,
ONE DAY I'LL EAT HIM UP,
(THIS MAN'S A GONER)
ONE DAY I'LL EAT HIM UP,
(ONE MORE TIME)
ONE DAY I'LL EAT HIM UP!

*As she starts to go there is the sound of an alarm. She gives her stomach a thump. The alarm stops. The ticking continues.*

*(CROCKETTES DANCE)*

MUSIC CONTINUES SEGUES INTO

SCENE FIVE.

*The Mermaids' lagoon, dominated by Marooner's Rock. The scene is bathed in moonlight.*

*A MERMAID is seated on the rock combing her hair and singing to herself.*

MERMAID: SAILOR SAILOR FAR FROM HOME,
COME LISTEN TO MY SONG,
NEVER THE SEAS AGAIN TO ROAM,
YOU'VE BEEN AWAY TOO LONG.

SAILOR SAILOR STAY WITH ME,
THE WIND IS WILD AND STRONG,
THERE IS A PLACE BENEATH THE SEA,
THAT IS WHERE YOU BELONG.

*She carries on humming and, as she does PETER and WENDY appear on the rock.*

WENDY: Oh, Peter! A real mermaid!

PETER: Don't get too close, Wendy. They are cruel creatures. She could pull you under the water and drown you. That's why she's singing. If there is a ship close by the sailors will hear her and come too close to the rock, then. (He makes a gesture with his hand indicating a sinking ship).

WENDY: If that's the case, why haven't the pirates all drowned?

PETER: Pirates are such coarse creatures. Her song doesn't get through to them.

WENDY: Aren't you afraid of them?

PETER: I'm afraid of nothing.

WENDY: She's so beautiful.

PETER: Huh! There's the danger. What's that?

*The MERMAID has stopped humming and, after a second of listening, she disappears, with a splash, off the rock just as a rowboat appears with SMEE steering, STARKEY rowing, and TIGER LILY a bound prisoner.*

SMEE: AVAST, BELAY, YO HO, HEAVE TO,
A PIRATING WE GO,
AND IF WE'RE PARTED BY A SHOT,
WE'RE SURE TO MEET BELOW.

BOTH: YO HO, YO HO, THE PIRATE LIFE,
THE FLAG OF SKULL AND BONES,
A MERRY HOUR, A HEMPEN ROPE,
AND HEY FOR DAVY JONES.

*They repeat the last two lines of the song until the boat strikes the rock and SMEE is hurled onto STARKEY.*

SMEE: Luff, you spalpeen, luff!

*They recover their balance.*

SMEE: Now what we have got to do here is hoist this here Indian princess onto the rock and leave her there to drown.

TIGER LILY: Huh!

*The PIRATES drag her onto the rock.*

SMEE: No mewling, no whining.

TIGER LILY: Huh!

Marooner's Rock - The mermaid's lagoon

SMEE: Oh, defiant to the end are we, missy? We'll see how you feel, my dear, when the water's lapping your chin. Not so rough, Starkey. Roughish but not quite so rough.

STARKEY: Captain's orders.

WENDY: Poor girl.

SMEE: What was that?

PETER: *(In HOOK's voice)* Ahoy there, you lubbers!

SMEE: It's the cap'n.

STARKEY: We've put the redskin on the rock, Captain.

PETER: Set her free.

SMEE: But, Captain...

PETER: Cut her bonds or I'll plunge my hook in you.

SMEE: This is mighty queer.

STARKEY: But we'd best follow the captain's orders.

*They untie TIGER LILY who darts off over the rock and disappears just as HOOK appears from the other side.*

HOOK: Ahoy there.

SMEE: Ahoy there, cap'n.

STARKEY: Captain, is all well?

SMEE: What's up, cap'n? You do look gloomy.

HOOK: The game is up, lads, those boys have found a mother.

STARKEY: Oh, evil day!

| | |
|---|---|
| SMEE: | What's a mother? |
| WENDY: | He doesn't know! |
| HOOK: | What was that? |
| STARKEY: | One of them mermaids. |
| HOOK: | Dost not know, Smee? What a mother is? |
| STARKEY: | Maybe she's hanging about to protect Peter. |
| SMEE: | Captain, could we not kidnap the boys' mother and make her our mother? |
| HOOK: | Oh, Smee, don't be such a… princely scheme, Smee. We will seize the children, make them walk the plank, and Wendy shall be our mother. What say you, bullies? |

*WENDY is about to protest but PETER puts his finger to his lips.*

| | |
|---|---|
| STARKEY: | There's my hand on it. |
| SMEE: | And mine. |
| HOOK: | And there's my hook. But I had forgot. Where's the prisoner? |
| SMEE: | We let her go, cap'n. |
| STARKEY: | That's right, captain. We let her go. |
| HOOK: | Blundering blistering blithering bluebottles! You what? |
| STARKEY: | Twas your orders, cap'n. |
| SMEE: | You called over the water to us, "Set her free," you said, "or I'll sink my hook into you." Those were your very words, captain. |

| | | |
|---|---|---|
| HOOK: | Brimstone and gall! What cozening is here? I gave no such order. | |
| SMEE: | Then the rock is haunted for we both did hear you. | |
| STARKEY: | Aye that we did. | |
| HOOK: | Haunted? | |
| SMEE: | Perhaps the spirit of some long drowned sailor man. | |
| HOOK: | You think so? Spirit that haunts this dark lagoon to-night, dost hear me? | |
| PETER: | Odds, bobs, hammer and tongs, I hear you. | |

*SMEE and STARKEY draw closer to each other for comfort. HOOK is distinctly startled.*

| | | |
|---|---|---|
| HOOK: | Who are you, stranger. Speak. |
| PETER: | I am Jas Hook, captain of the Jolly Roger. |
| HOOK: | No, no, you are not. |
| PETER: | Brimstone and gall, say that again and I'll cast anchor in you. |
| HOOK: | If you are Hook, come tell me, who am I? |
| PETER: | A codfish. No more than a codfish. |
| HOOK: | A codfish? |
| SMEE: | Have we been captained all this time by a codfish? |
| STARKEY: | It's lowering to our pride, that's what it is. |
| HOOK: | A codfish am I? We'll see about that. Spirit that haunts this rock. have you another name? |
| PETER: | Ay, ay. |

| | |
|---|---|
| HOOK: | Vegetable? |
| PETER: | No. |
| HOOK: | Mineral? |
| PETER: | No. |
| HOOK: | Animal? |
| PETER: | Yes. |
| HOOK: | Man? |
| PETER: | No. |
| HOOK: | Boy? |
| PETER: | Yes. |
| HOOK: | Ordinary boy? |
| PETER: | No! |
| HOOK: | Wonderful boy? |
| PETER: | Yes! |

*HOOK excitedly mimes for SMEE to go around the rock and surprise PETER from behind and for STARKEY to mind the boat. This they do.*

| | |
|---|---|
| HOOK: | Are you in England? |
| PETER: | No. |
| HOOK: | Are you here? |
| PETER: | Yes. Well, who am I? |
| HOOK: | I really can't think. |

PETER: Do you give up?

HOOK: I give up.

PETER: I am Peter Pan!

*SMEE tackles PETER and is in turn tackled by WENDY. In the melee HOOK strikes and is about to strike again when he stops dead as he hears the tick tick tick of the clock.*

HOOK: Smee! Into the boat! Quick! Row! Row for my life!

MUSIC

*The boat quickly moves off to disappear followed by the CROCODILE doing a pas de chat over the water.*

WENDY: *(Over the prostrate PETER)* Peter! Peter!

PETER: What is it?

WENDY: We must go. Look, the water is rising. The rock is getting smaller.

PETER: Yes.

WENDY: Shall we swim or shall we fly?

PETER: Wendy, do you think you could swim or fly to the island without me?

WENDY: You know I couldn't, Peter. I'm only a beginner.

PETER: Hook wounded me twice. I can neither swim nor fly. Look how the water is rising.

WENDY: We will both be drowned.

PETER: Yes, I suppose so.

WENDY: Aren't you afraid?

PETER: I don't think so.

WENDY: I am. Terribly afraid.

PETER: Don't be. Don't be. To die will be an awfully big adventure.

MUSIC SWELLS AS CURTAIN DROPS.

# ACT TWO.

## SCENE ONE.

*Part of the forest. The INDIANS perform a war-dance which reaches a climax just as TIGER LILY runs on.*

TIGER LILY: Hold, braves! Oh, great chief, my father, pirates take prisoner Tiger Lily but Tiger Lily saved by Peter Pan.

*Whoops from the BRAVES. The CHIEF raises his hand to silence them.*

CHIEF: Peter Pan brave. Peter Pan smart alec, heap big clever dick. Will smoke peace pipe with Peter Pan. No more make war.

TIGER LILY: Pirates make war, kill Peter Pan, take boys prisoner, keep boys' mother. Make pirates' mother. I hear him say on rock.

*Groans from the Braves.*

CHIEF: We guard'um den. Pirates come, we kill, take'um scalp. Chief Great Big Little Panther has spoken.

*More whoops and hollers as they all dance off to guard the boys' den. As they go, LIGHTS come up behind scrim to reveal*

## SCENE TWO.

*The Home under the Ground.*

*It is a large cave with entrances from between the roots of trees. There is bedding on the ground large enough to accommodate all the boys, possibly head to toe, except for Michael who sleeps in a basket hung fairly high. Brightly coloured toadstools or pumpkins form the seating and the table is a board on a sawn-off tree trunk. There is a small curtained alcove which is Tink's bed chamber and from which comes a glow indicating she is in. All the BOYS are present and in the depths of gloom.*

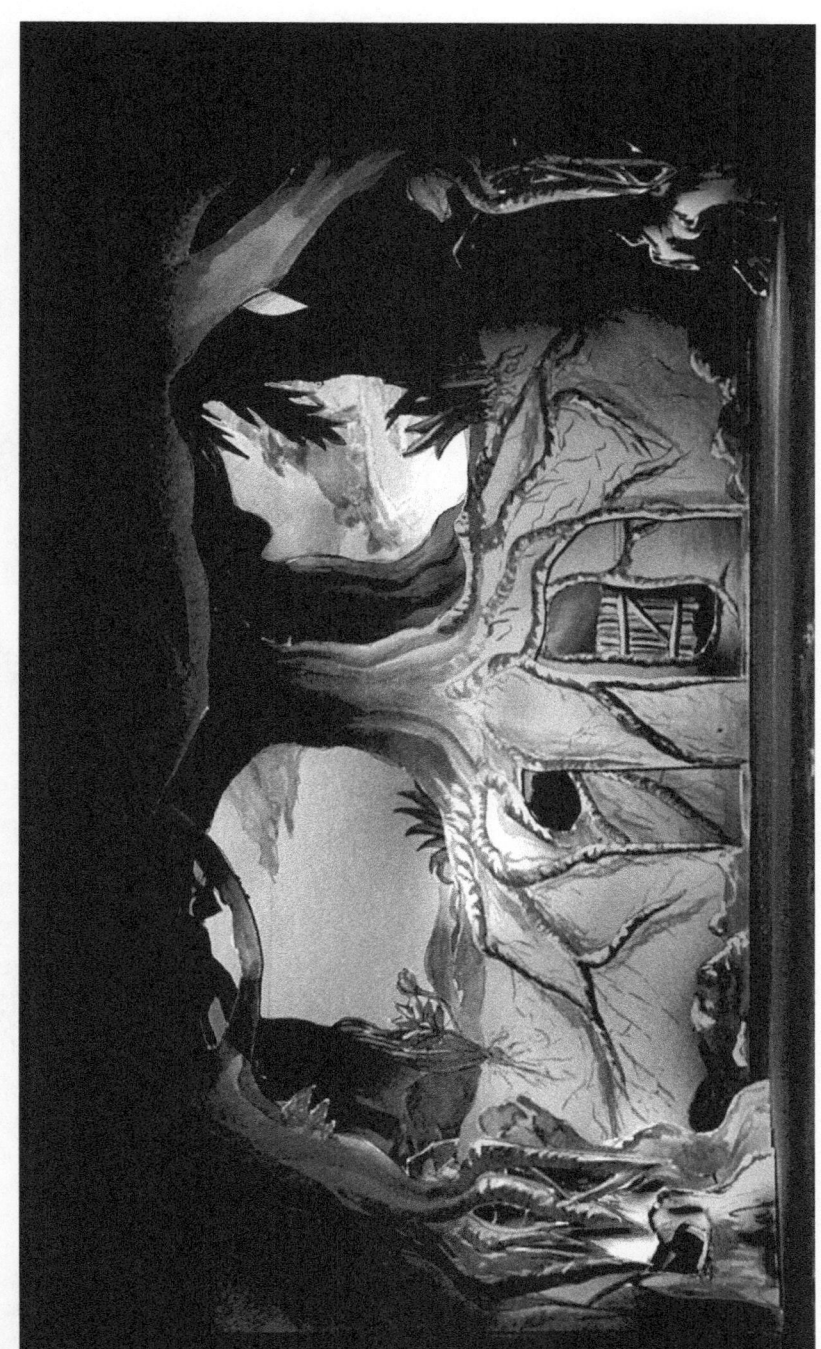

The home underground

TOOTLES: *(Big sigh)* I do wish Peter and Wendy would come. It's been ages.

1st TWIN: Yes, I'm hungry.

2nd TWIN: So am I.

TWINS: We're both hungry.

SLIGHTLY: Do you think something could have happened to them?

CURLY: Maybe we should go and look for them.

NIBS: Yes, or we'll never get to eat.

TOOTLES: Wait! Listen!

*Sounds of war whoops.*

SLIGHTLY: Indians.

CURLY: On the warpath!

NIBS: Do you think they've got Peter?

TOOTLES: Shhh!

*They all listen. There is no sound from above.*

JOHN: Do you think they've gone?

TOOTLES: *(Shaking his head)* It's a trap. They're only pretending to have gone. I know about Indians.

SLIGHTLY: Huh!

TOOTLES: If you don't believe me, stick your head out and see. You'll come back without any hair.

1st TWIN: What're we going to do?

2nd TWIN:   If only Peter was here.

*And, as if to answer his prayer, there is the sound of crowing and, in a second, PETER, with another loud crow, emerges from one hole and WENDY from another.*

PETER:   Greetings, men, I'm back!

*Loud cheers.*

TWINS:   We're hungry!

WENDY:   Well, we'll soon see about that. Slightly, lay the table for supper please.

SLIGHTLY:   I did it last time.

PETER:   No arguments, do as your mother says. Oh, boys, we've had such an adventure.

TOOTLES:   Tell! Tell!

*SLIGHTLY mimes laying the table as they all listen to PETER's adventure.*

PETER:   Your mother and I met Captain Hook and some of his men on Marooner's Rock. They had Tiger Lily a prisoner but I freed her and then we fought the pirates and Hook wounded me twice before he escaped.

WENDY:   And we were left marooned because Peter couldn't swim nor fly and...

*PETER clears his throat.*

WENDY:   Sorry. Do go on. No, Slightly, how many more times? Forks on the left, knives on the right. *(She rearranges the imaginary cutlery).*

PETER:   The water was rising, rising...

1st TWIN:   Oh, anguish!

| | |
|---|---|
| 2nd TWIN: | How mortifying. |
| PETER: | Well, it nearly was, but then, because I am such a splendid playfellow when occasion arises, the mermaids came to our rescue and we swam back to shore on their backs. |
| TOOTLES: | That's very un-mermaid like behaviour, I mean for mermaids. |
| PETER: | A little less noise there if you please. |
| JOHN: | That's my line. |
| PETER: | You too or you go to bed without any supper. Where was I? Oh, yes, and because I rescued Tiger Lily from the pirates, I have been made Great White Father and Chief Great Big Little Panther and his braves are right this very minute guarding our house. |
| NIBS: | So pirates better watch their step. |
| PETER: | Yes indeed. |
| WENDY: | Boys, supper is on the table. |

*With much yelling, jostling, shoving and pushing, the BOYS seat themselves around the table.*

| | |
|---|---|
| JOHN: | Can I sit in Peter's chair? |
| WENDY: | In your father's chair? Certainly not. |
| JOHN: | He's not really our father. He didn't even know how to be a father until I showed him. |
| 2nd TWIN: | I complain of John! |
| TOOTLES: | Would anyone like to see me do a trick? |
| ALL: | No! |

| | |
|---|---|
| TOOTLES: | I didn't think you would. |
| CURLY: | I complain of Tootles! |
| SLIGHTLY: | I complain of Nibs! |
| NIBS: | I complain of Slightly! |
| WENDY: | Oh dear, I sometimes think it would have better to have remained a spinster and not had children at all. What's wrong, Peter? |
| PETER: | It is only pretend isn't it? That I'm their father. |
| WENDY: | Oh yes. |
| JOHN: | Bun fight! |

*Uproar from the BOYS.*

| | |
|---|---|
| PETER: | A little less noise there if you please. |
| WENDY: | Peter, what are your exact feelings for me? |
| PETER: | What a silly question. You are so puzzling. Tinker Bell is just the same. There is something or other she wants me to be but she says it's not my mother. |
| WENDY: | No, indeed, it isn't. |
| PETER: | Then what is it? |
| WENDY: | That's not for a lady to tell. |

*The alcove curtain opens slightly and TINK's merry laugh is heard.*

| | |
|---|---|
| WENDY: | She called you a silly ass again and I almost agree with her. |
| PETER: | Boys, have you finished? |

*CHORUS of "Yeses"*

PETER: Then into bed with you and Wendy will tell us a story.

*As there was to the table so there is a wild noisy scramble for the bed. PETER and WENDY draw up stools.*

WENDY: Well, once upon a time there was a gentleman...

CURLY: I wish he'd been a lady.

NIBS: I wish he'd been a white rat.

SLIGHTLY: I complain of Nibs!

WENDY: Quiet! Do you want to hear this story or don't you? Well then. The gentleman's name was Mr Darling and the lady's name was Mrs Darling.

JOHN: I knew them!

NIBS: I complain...ouch!

*As TOOTLES clouts him with a pillow.*

MICHAEL: I think I knewed them too.

WENDY: They were married you know; and what do you think they had?

NIBS: White rats.

WENDY: No, they had three descendants

NIBS: Aren't white rats descendants?

WENDY: Er...ye-es, but only of other white rats. The Darlings had children and these three children had a faithful nurse called Nana.

MICHAEL: What a funny name.

WENDY: But one night Mr Darling... or was it Mrs Darling?... was angry with Nana and chained her up in the yard; so all the children flew away. They flew away to the Never Land where the lost boys are.

CURLY: I just thought they did; I don't know how it is, but I just thought they did.

TOOTLES: Oh, Wendy, was one of the lost boys called Tootles?

WENDY: Yes, he was.

TOOTLES: I'm in a story! Nibs, I'm in a story! Everybody...

*He is silenced by a severe pillow thumping.*

WENDY: But the children knew that their mother would always leave the windows open for them to fly back so they stayed for years and had a lovely time.

JOHN: Didn't they ever go back?

PETER: Wendy, you are wrong about mothers. I thought like you about windows so I stayed away for moons and moons and then I flew back. But the window was barred for my mother had forgotten all about me and there was another little boy sleeping in my bed.

JOHN: Wendy, let us go back! At once!

WENDY: Are you sure mothers are like that?

PETER: Yes.

WENDY: *(Holding out her hands)* John! Michael!

1st TWIN: *(Alarmed)* you're not going to leave us!

2nd TWIN: Are you?

WENDY: I must.

NIBS: Not to-night.

WENDY: Yes, at once. Peter, will you make the arrangements?

PETER: If you wish it.

*He ascends his tree.*

CURLY: We won't let you go!

WENDY: Tootles, I appeal to you.

TOOTLES: *(Shadow boxing wildly)* I am just Tootles and nobody minds me, but the first who does not behave to Wendy I will blood him severely.

*PETER returns.*

PETER: Wendy, the braves will guide you through the woods, then Tinker bell will take you across the sea.

*There is a shrill tinkle from the boudoir.*

PETER: Tink, get up and dress at once.

WENDY: I have an idea. Why don't you all come with us? I'm sure I can get my father and mother to adopt you.

NIBS: But won't they think us rather a handful?

WENDY: Oh, no, it will only mean having a few beds in the drawing room

1st TWIN: Peter...

2nd TWIN: ...may we go?

SLIGHTLY: May we?

PETER: All right. But I won't be going.

WENDY: Peter!

CURLY: Peter's not coming!

TOOTLES: But why, Peter?

PETER: Because I just want always to be a little boy and have fun. So no fuss, no blubbing, I just hope you all like your new mother, that's all. Are you ready, Tink? Then lead the way.

*TINK darts for a tree but gets no further than the hole. Suddenly there is a fearful ruckus above.*

PETER: *(Drawing his dagger)* Pirates! They've attacked!

*They all wait, staring upwards. After a while there is silence.*

PETER: All is over.

WENDY: But who has won?

PETER: If the Indians have won they will beat the tom-tom. it is their signal of victory.

*For a moment longer they listen in silence before they hear the sound of the tom-tom.*

PETER: The tom-tom! An Indian victory. *(He sheathes his dagger).*

*There are cheers from the BOYS.*

PETER: You are quite safe now, Wendy. Boys, good-bye. *(He sits on his stool and produces his pipes).*

*The BOYS are already disappearing up their respective trees but WENDY lingers. PETER starts to play his pipes.*

WENDY: Peter...are you sure you won't be coming with us?

PETER:   Quite sure, thank you.

WENDY:   Then it's good-bye.

PETER:   Yes.

WENDY:   Peter...

PETER:   Yes?

WENDY:   *(Indicating a seashell situated somewhere close to his tree)* You won't forget to take your medicine will you?

PETER:   No.

WENDY:   It's right here.

PETER:   Yes.

WENDY:   Peter...

PETER:   Yes?

WENDY:   I just wanted to say...

PETER:
WENDY:
WE'VE BEEN LUCKY, YOU AND I,
TO KNOW EACH OTHER.
WE'VE HAD GOOD TIMES
AND ADVENTURES QUITE A FEW
BUT THE MOMENT'S COME WHEN WE ALWAYS KNEW
WE'D HAVE TO SAY GOOD-BYE.

I'LL RELIVE WHEN I AM OLD,
MEMORIES THAT WILL GLEAM LIKE GOLD,
OF THE WONDERFUL TIME WE HAD TOGETHER.
THESE FEELINGS MAY BE NEW
YET IN YOUR HEART YOU KNOW IT,
I UNDERSTAND THE REASON YOU
STILL FIND IT HARD TO SHOW IT.

| | |
|---|---|
| PETER: | LUCKY OLD YOU, |
| WENDY: | LUCKY OLD ME, |
| BOTH: | LUCKY OLD US DON'T YOU AGREE? |
| | TO HAVE HAD SUCH A WONDERFUL TIME |
| | TO-GETHER. |
| | |
| WENDY: | I THINK WE KNEW IT WOULDN'T LAST, |
| | WHY DID IT HAVE TO GO SO FAST? |
| PETER: | WE WERE HAVING A REALLY GREAT TIME |
| | TOGETHER. |
| | WE'VE BEEN THE BEST OF FRIENDS, |
| BOTH: | I HATE TO SEE US BREAK UP, |
| WENDY: | BUT ALL GOOD THINGS MUST HAVE AN END, |
| | I GUESS IT'S TIME TO WAKE UP. |
| | |
| | READY TO GO, FACING THE DAY, |
| | TIME DOESN'T WAIT, LIFE'S NOT ALL PLAY, |
| PETER: | BUT WE DID HAVE A WONDERFUL TIME, |
| | TOGETHER. |
| | |
| WENDY: | The truth is, Peter, I suppose I'm homesick. There are so many things I miss. And, Peter, I do want to grow up. I don't want to be a little girl for always. I do want to be a woman. |
| | |
| PETER: | No! |
| | |
| | IT DOESN'T HAVE TO BE, |
| | THIS LAND THAT WE CALL NEVER, |
| | IS PARADISE FOR YOU AND ME, |
| | SO WHY NOT STAY FOREVER? |
| | |
| WENDY: | NO IT'S NOT TRUE, LIVING IN DREAMS, |
| | NOTHING IS REAL, NOT WHAT IT SEEMS, |
| | THOUGH WE DID HAVE A WONDERFUL TIME, |
| | YES WE DID HAVE A WONDERFUL TIME. |
| | A GLORIOUS |
| | |
| PETER: | FABULOUS, |
| | |
| WENDY: | WONDERFUL, |

PETER:        UNFORGETTABLE TIME,

BOTH:         TOGETHER.

WENDY:        Good-bye, Peter.

*PETER waves an airy hand and WENDY goes. He wanders down to his stool and sits head in hands, then he looks up.*

PETER:        No, I won't cry. No matter what, I won't cry.

                    ALL MY LIFE, YOU'LL BE IN MY DREAMS,
                    I'LL WONDER WHEN I WAKE UP
                    WHERE YOU ARE, HOW COULD YOU LEAVE ME THIS WAY?
                    THOUGH THE YEARS WILL FLY,
                    THE MEMORIES WILL ALWAYS STAY.

                    SAY YOU'LL REMEMBER ME YOUR WHOLE LIFE THROUGH,
                    I WILL KNOW THE REASON I BELIEVE IN YOU,
                    AND THOUGH WE ARE APART I KNOW WE'LL FIND,
                    FOREVER IS A LONG LONG TIME.

                    HOURS AND HOURS, SLIPPING AWAY
                    WE COULD HAVE HAD TOMORROW,
                    YOUNG AND FREE. HOW COULD YOU LEAVE ME THIS WAY?
                    THOUGH THE YEARS WILL FLY,
                    I KNOW WE'LL MEET AGAIN SOME DAY.

                    SAY YOU'LL REMEMBER ME YOUR WHOLE LIFE THROUGH,
                    I WILL KNOW THE REASON I BELIEVE IN YOU,
                    I'LL HAVE THE MEMORIES YOU LEFT BEHIND,
                    FOREVER IS A LONG LONG TIME.

                    MORE THAN JUST A FRIEND,
                    HOW CAN I BELIEVE THIS THE END?
                    THERE'S NO WAY I CAN PRETEND,
                    YOU GAVE ME YOUR KISS, AND HOW I'M GOING

>     TO MISS YOU.
>
>     SAY YOU'LL REMEMBER ME YOUR WHOLE LIFE THOUGH,
>     I WILL KNOW THE REASON I BELIEVE IN YOU,
>     WE'LL HAVE THE MEMORIES WE'VE LEFT BEHIND,
>     FOREVER IS A LONG LONG TIME,
>     JUST SAY YOUR LOVE FOR ME WILL NEVER DIE,
>     FOREVER IS A LONG LONG TIME.

PETER *throws himself on the bed and is immediately asleep just as* HOOK *appears at the entrance of Slightly's tree. But he can get no further than that. He glares at the sleeping* PETER *and snarls wickedly. Then he notices the medicine and, with a wicked chuckle, produces a bottle of poison and pours a few drops into the medicine. Then he disappears the way he came.*

*At the same time a flash of light appears from another tree as* TINK *darts into the room.*

PETER: *(Stirring)* Who's there? *(He sits up as* TINK *lets out a stream of talk)* The redskins were defeated? Wendy and the boys captured by the pirates! I'll rescue her! I'll rescue her!

*He runs for his tree but pauses when he sees his medicine.* TINK *has also seen it and settles on the shell tinkling a warning.*

PETER: It's my medicine, Tink. Poisoned? Who could have poisoned it? I promised Wendy I'd take it. *(He lifts the shell)* Tink! You've drunk my medicine!

*She flutters strangely about the room answering him now in a very faint tinkle.*

PETER: It was poisoned and you drank it to save my life. Tink, dear, Tink, are you dying?

TINK *retires to her boudoir where her light flickers ominously.*

PETER: Her light is growing faint, and if it goes out, that

means she is dead! Her voice is so low I can scarcely tell what she is saying. She says...she says she thinks she could get well again if children believed in fairies. *(He throws out his arms)* Do you believe in fairies? Say quick that you believe! If you believe clap your hands! *(He urges them on if necessary)* Oh thank you! Thank you! Thank you! *(TINK is saved)* And now to rescue Wendy!

MUSIC.

### SCENE THREE.

*Part of the forest. The CHILDREN, bound captives, being hauled away by the PIRATES. SMEE leads the way.*

*As the last one disappears, HOOK enters with JOHN and WENDY but they have not got very far when there is the ominous TICK TICK TICK so dreaded by HOOK. With a shriek he takes off after his men completely forgetting his captives.*

*There is a second and then TIGER LILY appears.*

| | |
|---|---|
| WENDY: | Was that you making that noise? |
| TIGER LILY: | *(Nods)* You come with Tiger Lily. |
| JOHN: | Wendy! We're saved! |
| WENDY: | No we're not. |
| JOHN: | No? |
| WENDY: | Have you forgotten Michael? The boys? They're in terrible danger. |
| JOHN: | *(Somewhat shamefaced)* Sorry. |
| WENDY: | We have to rescue them. Tiger Lily, where are your braves? They could help. |
| TIGER LILY: | No braves. |

JOHN: You mean they're all dead?

*TIGER LILY shakes her head.*

TIGER LILY: HIDE UM HEAD, HIDE UM FACE,
LOSE UM FIGHT, BIG DISGRACE,
NOT GONE TO HAPPY HUNTING GROUND,
GONE TO BED INSTEAD.

JOHN: Oh dear!

TIGER LILY: NURSE UM CUTS, NURSE UM BUMPS,
WHAT A SIGHT, HEAP BIG LUMPS,

JOHN: THERE'S NOT AN INDIAN TO BE FOUND?
TIGER LILY: ARE THEIR FACES RED!

WENDY: WHAT ARE WE GOING TO DO
TO GET AWAY FROM THIS PIRATE CREW?
JOHN: WE WILL END UP SKULL AND BONES
IN THAT LOCKER OWNED BY DAVY JONES.

TIGER LILY: NO SAY THAT, NO GIVE IN,
KEEP UP CHIN, YOU WILL WIN,
JOHN: I GUESS WHERE LIFE IS THERE IS HOPE.
TIGER LILY: BETTER HOPE THAN MOPE.

PIRATES THINK PIRATES STRONG,
NO GOT BRAINS, THINK'UM WRONG.
SMART REDSKINS SET'UM HEAP BIG TRAP,
PIRATES ALL GO SPLAT.

WENDY: EASY FOR YOU TO SAY,
I'VE GOT A FEELING TO-DAY'S THE DAY,
JOHN: WHEN WE ALL WILL WALK THE PLANK,
THEN IT'S FIVE FATHOMS DOWN ALL COLD AND DANK.

TIGER LILY: No!
MAKE UM SONG, MAKE UM DANCE,
PAINT UM FACE, TAKE UM CHANCE,

WENDY/
JOHN:                WE'LL FIND A WAY TO BEAT THAT CROOK,
                    WATCH OUT CAPTAIN HOOK!

*They do a war dance during which they are joined by some of the injured and bandaged BRAVES. HOOK sneakingly returns. TIGER LILY and the BRAVES see him and flee. HOOK creeps up behind JOHN and WENDY and, as they finish their dance, he claps a hand on one shoulder, his hook on another.*

HOOK:               Gotcha!

BLACKOUT.

## SCENE FOUR.

*The pirate ship.*

*SMEE, on the main deck, is seated on a barrel in front of his sewing machine, possibly running up another version of The Jolly Roger or merely repairing a pirate shirt or two.*

*JUKES is fast asleep against a bulwark and NOODLER is on the poop deck raking the seas with a telescope. HOOK is pacing.*

HOOK:               How still the night is. Now is the hour when children in their homes are abed. Compare them with the children on this boat about to walk the plank. Split my infinitives but tis my hour of triumph.

*He dances a few hornpipe steps but stops dead as SMEE rips a piece of material. HOOK feels his trousers but, seemingly satisfied nothing untoward has happened, continues.*

HOOK:               And yet some spirit compels me now to make my dying speech lest, when dying, there may be no time for it. O fame, fame, thou glittering bauble, all mortals envy me, yet better for Captain Hook to have had less ambition. *(Another rending sound and HOOK almost leaps out of his trousers before continuing)* No little children love me. I am told they play at Peter Pan and the strongest always chooses to be Peter.

The Pirate Ship

They force the baby to be Hook. The baby! That is where the canker gnaws. Tis said they find Smee lovable. Poor pathetic Smee, a happy smile upon his face because he thinks they fear him. How can I break it to him that they think he's lovable?

*Another piece of material is ripped. This time HOOK gives STARKEY a kick to wake him up and inspect for damage. Eight bells strikes. STARKEY assures HOOK that all is well just as JUKES appears from below.*

HOOK: Are all the prisoners chained so they can't fly away?

JUKES: Ay ay, Captain.

HOOK: Then hoist them up.

STARKEY: *(At the door of the cabin)* Tumble up, you ungentlemanly lubbers.

*As the BOYS emerge and are tumbled about by the rumbustious PIRATES, HOOK produces a pack of cards and seats himself on a barrel.*

HOOK: Quiet, you dogs! Or I'll cast anchor in you. So. Now then, you bullies, six of you walk the plank to-night, but I have room for two cabin-boys. Which of you is it to be?

TOOTLES: I don't think my mother would like me to be a pirate. Would your mother like you to be a pirate, Slightly?

SLIGHTLY: No, I don't think my mother would like me to be a pirate. Twin would your mother...?

HOOK: Stow the gab! *(To JOHN)* You, boy, you look as though you have a bit of pluck in you. Didst never want to be a pirate, my hearty?

JOHN: Would we still be respectful subjects of the king?

HOOK: You would have to swear, "Down with the King".

JOHN: Then I refuse.

MICHAEL: And I refuse.

HOOK: No one asked you.

MICHAEL: I still refuse.

HOOK: That seals your doom. Bring up their mother.

*WENDY is brought on and thrown at HOOK's feet.*

HOOK: So, my proud beauty, you are to see your children walk the plank. Silence all for a mother's last words to her children.

WENDY: Dear boys, these are my last words; I feel I have a message to you from your real mothers and it is this, "We hope our sons will die like English gentlemen".

TOOTLES: I am going to do what my mother hopes. What are you going to do, Twin?

1st TWIN: What my mother hopes. John, what are...?

HOOK: Tie her up! Ready the plank!

*WENDY is roped to the mast and the plank is pushed out but, as HOOK raises his claw suddenly there is heard the ominous tick tick tick of the crocodile. All eyes turn from the plank to HOOK as the cards fly in all directions and the brave pirate cowers by the barrel. Out of respect for their captain the PIRATES close their eyes just as PETER appears over the side of the ship. It is NOODLER who sees him but, before he can raise the alarm, JOHN's hand is around his mouth, TOOTLES has one arm, NIBS the other, and there is a TWIN for each leg as PETER delivers a mighty blow with the hilt of his dagger. The unfortunate pirate is bundled overboard.*

SLIGHTLY: One.

*PETER slips into the cabin. The PIRATES open their eyes.*

STARKEY: It's gone, captain. There's not a sound.

HOOK: *(Pulling himself together)* Then here's to Johnny Plank.

> AVAST, BELAY, THE ENGLISH BRIG,
> WE QUICKLY TOOK AND SANK,
> AND FOR A WARNING TO THE CREW
> WE MADE THEM WALK THE PLANK.

CHORUS: YO HO, YO HO, THE FRISKY BOARD,
YOU WALKS ALONG IT SO,
TILL IT GOES DOWN AND YOU GOES DOWN
TO TOORAL LOORAL LO!

BOYS: RULE BRITANNIA, BRITANNIA RULES THE WAVES,
BRITONS NEVER NEVER NEVER SHALL BE SLAVES.

HOOK: Stow that, you landlubbers. Do you want a touch of the cat before you walk the plank? Fetch the cat, Jukes. It's in the cabin.

JUKES: Ay ay, sir.

HOOK: YO HO HO THE SCRATCHING CAT,
IT'S TAILS ARE NINE YOU KNOW,
AND WHEN THEY'VE WRIT UPON YOUR BACK,
YOU'RE FIT TO...(EAT A CROW)

*There is a loud crowing from the cabin.*

HOOK: What was that?

SLIGHTLY: Two.

*CECCO runs into the cabin and comes out twice as fast.*

HOOK: What's the matter with Bill Jukes?

| | |
|---|---|
| CECCO: | The matter with Bill Jukes is he's dead. |
| HOOK: | Bill Jukes dead? |
| CECCO: | The cabin is as black as a pit, but there's something terrible in there, the thing you heard a doodle-dooing. |
| HOOK: | Cecco, go in and fetch me out that doodle-doo. |
| CECCO: | No, captain, no! |
| HOOK: | *(Advancing on him)* Did you say you would go? |

*CECCO goes. All listen. There is a screech then a crow.*

| | |
|---|---|
| SLIGHTLY: | Three. |
| HOOK: | 'Sdeath and oddfish, who is to bring me out that doodle-doo? |
| STARKEY: | Wait till Cecco comes out. |
| HOOK: | Ah, did I hear you volunteer, Starkey? |

*STARKEY claps his hand over his mouth. Why did he open it?*

| | |
|---|---|
| HOOK: | Well, did I? |
| STARKEY: | No, by thunder! |
| HOOK: | My hook thinks you did. |
| STARKEY: | I'll swing before I go in there. |
| HOOK: | So, mutiny is it? Shake hands, Starkey. |

*The hook follows STARKEY until he jumps overboard.*

| | |
|---|---|
| SLIGHTLY: | Four. |
| HOOK: | I will bring out the doodle-doo myself. |

*With a lighted lantern he enters the cabin and immediately staggers out again.*

HOOK: Something blew out the light.

SMEE: S-s-s-some-thing? What of Cecco?

HOOK: As dead as Bill Jukes.

*There is a cheer from the BOYS. HOOK swings on them.*

HOOK: So you like it, do you? Well here is a notion. Smee? In with them. Let them fight the doodle-doo for their lives. If they kill him, we are so much the better; if he kills them we are none the worse.

*Affecting fear the BOYS are herded into the cabin.*

HOOK: I cannot bear to watch.

SMEE: Nor me.

*They turn their backs. PETER creeps out of the cabin, releases WENDY and, using her cloak. Takes her place. WENDY disappears into the cabin. PETER crows.*

SMEE: The doodle-doo has killed them all!

HOOK: I've thought it out, there is a Jonah aboard and it's a girl Jonah. Never was luck on a pirate ship with a woman on board. We'll throw her overboard.

SMEE: There's none can save you now, missy.

PETER: Oh, yes there is.

SMEE: Oh no there's not.

PETER: Oh yes there is.

SMEE: And who might that be then?

PETER: *(Throwing off the cloak)* Peter Pan the avenger!

HOOK: Cleave him to the brisket!

*The BOYS, all armed, come rushing and yelling out of the cabin. HOOK turns on them.*

HOOK: Back! Back, you mice! This is Hook you're dealing with. How do you like him?

*The BOYS stop in awe of the flashing hook.*

PETER: Put up your swords, boys. This man is mine! *(He gets a sword from one of the boys).*

HOOK: *(Turns back)* So, Pan, this is all your doing.

PETER: Ay, Jas Hook, all my doing.

HOOK: Proud and insolent youth, prepare to meet thy doom.

PETER: Dark and sinister man, have at thee.

MUSIC

*They fight. HOOK's sword flies from his grasp and as he kneels to retrieve it, PETER steps on the blade.*

BOYS: Now, Peter, now!

*PETER picks up the sword by the blade and presents the hilt to his enemy.*

HOOK: Tis some fiend fighting me! Pan, who and what art thou?

PETER: I'm youth, I'm joy, I'm a little bird that has broken out of the egg.

HOOK: To't again.

*HOOK, realising he is never going to win, suddenly backs off.*

HOOK: I'll fire the powder magazine! It will take two minutes for the ship to be blown to pieces.

*He disappears into the cabin.*

CHILDREN: Peter! Save us!

*But PETER merely holds up his hand for quiet. In the silence can be heard the tick tick of the crocodile. Suddenly there is an unearthly screech and HOOK comes flying out of the hold, leaps onto the plank and disappears over the side. He is followed by the CROCODILE who, as she reaches the side, turns back for a moment.*

CROC: Thank you, boys. I always said this man would be mine.

*She slides sinuously over the bulwarks to disappear after Hook.*

JOHN: Three cheers for Peter Pan. Hip hip...

BOYS: Hooray. etc.

WENDY: And now...for home.

## SCENE FIVE.

*The street outside the Darling home.*

*WENDY, JOHN, and MICHAEL wander on, looking for their own front door.*

WENDY: I think this is it.

JOHN: I'm not so sure. Do you remember it, Michael?

*MICHAEL shakes his head.*

WENDY: Well there's only one way to find out isn't there?

A London Street - The Darling Home

|          | We'll ring the bell. *(She does so)* and, whoever answers, if we don't know them, we'll just say, "Excuse me, we're looking for the Darling residence." All right? |
|---|---|
| JOHN: | I suppose so. |

*The door opens and LISA appears.*

| WENDY: | Excuse me... |
|---|---|
| LISA: | Why! It's Miss Wendy! And John! And Michael! You're back! |
| JOHN: | Do we know you? |
| LISA: | Of course you do. |
| MICHAEL: | Mother! |
| LISA: | Oh, you silly thing. I'm not your mother. Your mother... |

*TOOTLES appears.*

| LISA: | And who's this when it's at home? |
|---|---|
| WENDY: | Oh, this is Tootles. |
| LISA: | Well, tootle-do Tootles. You three come inside. |
| WENDY: | Oh, but Tootles is coming in with us. He's adopted you see. |
| LISA: | Oh. Really? |

*SLIGHTLY and NIBS appear.*

| LISA: | And who might these two be? |
|---|---|
| JOHN: | Oh, these are Slightly and Nibs. |

LISA: They're adopted too I suppose.

MICHAEL: Oh, yes!

*CURLY appears.*

LISA: Likewise?

*They all nod.*

*Finally the TWINS appear hand in hand.*

LISA: Now they're coming in pairs. Are there any more?

WENDY: We-ell...

*There is the sound of a joyful bark from inside and NANA comes out of the house. There is an immediate joyful reunion and NANA has a good sniff at all the newcomers. There are cries of "Nana! Nana!" from the DARLINGS.*

LISA: Heaven only knows what your mother and father are going to say. Still, they'll be that pleased to see you they might just overlook the extras.

WENDY: Boys, this is Nana. She is our nursemaid.

NANA: Woof woof.

*Everybody makes a fuss of NANA who enjoys it mightily.*

LISA: Well, you'd best all come in then.

*SMEE appears smiling happily and is about to troop in after the CHILDREN when LISA puts out a hand.*

LISA: And who might you be?

SMEE: Smee.

LISA: Yes, I know it's you, but who are you?

| | |
|---|---|
| SMEE: | I've just told you. Smee. |
| LISA: | I don't think you belong here at all. You can't even tell me who you are. |
| SMEE: | Smee! Smee! I'm Smee! |
| LISA: | Well, whoever you are, you're not a boy, so you can't come in. |

*And she slams the door, inadvertently leaving NANA outside as well. SMEE turns to look at NANA who puts her paws on his shoulders and gives his face a wash, steaming up his glasses so that he has to take them off and give them a good wipe, using the same handkerchief to wipe away the tear from his eye.*

| | |
|---|---|
| SMEE: | I don't know why it is, but nobody ever seems to want me. I wasn't wanted as a child you know. That's why I ran away and became a pirate. I never really wanted to be a pirate but at least they put up with me. |
| NANA: | Woof. |
| SMEE: | What? |
| NANA: | Woof woof. |
| SMEE: | Would you want me? |
| NANA: | Woof. |
| SMEE: | You would? And do you think you could put in a word for me... you know... in there? So maybe I could be adopted too? |
| NANA: | Woof. |
| SMEE: | Oh, Nana, you're a perfect darlin' of a dog, that you are. |

*If NANA were human she would blush. As it is she grows mighty skittish.*

SMEE: NOBODY NEEDS TO BE TOLD (WOOF WOOF),
A DOG AS NURSEMAID
DISPENSING THE FIRST AID'S
A PET WITH A HEART OF GOLD. (WOOF WOOF)

WHAT IF HER NOSE MIGHT BE COLD (WOOF WOOF)
AND OFTEN QUITE RUNNY?
SHE'S WARM AND SHE'S FUNNY
THE DOG WITH A HEART OF GOLD. (WOOF WOOF. WOOF WOOF)

SHE'S BRAVE, SHE'S CUTE,
SHE'S MOST ASTUTE
SHE HAS THE GENTLEST OF JAWS.
AND IF YOU'RE CHRONIC AND NEED A TONIC,
YOU'RE IN THE SAFEST OF PAWS. (WOOF WOOF)

A TREASURE NOT TO BE SOLD, (WOOF WOOF)
SHE'S ONE IN A MILLION,
YES, SOME SAY A TRILLION,
THIS DOG WITH THE HEART OF GOLD. (WOOF WOOF)

(AND I WISH SHE WERE MY MOTHER)

THIS DOG WITH A HEART OF GOLD. (WOOF WOOF WOOF WOOF)
ENCORE

NOBODY NEEDS TO BE TOLD,
A DOG AS NURSEMAID,
DISPENSING THE FIRST AID'S
A PET WITH A HEART OF GOLD.

WONDERFUL JUST TO BEHOLD, (WOOF WOOF)
WHO CARES ABOUT FLEAS WHEN
SO EAGER TO PLEASE SHE'S
THE DOG WITH A HEART OF GOLD. (WOOF WOOF, WOOF WOOF)

|         | SHE'S HIP, SHE'S BRILL, |
|---------|---|

                    SHE'S HIP, SHE'S BRILL,
                    SHE KNOWS THE DRILL,
                    SHE'LL SEE THAT IT ALL COMES RIGHT.
                    SO DON'T GET MANIC, NO NEED TO PANIC,
                    HER BARK IS WORSE THAN HER BITE.

RPT:          A TREASURE NOT TO BE SOLD.

                              SCENE SIX.

*The nursery, MRS DARLING asleep in a chair. The window is open. We hear the music of the LULLABY and she stirs, wakes, looks at the empty beds and sings...*

MRS DARL:    AT THE END OF THE RAINBOW FIND YOUR DREAMS.
                    STARLIGHT, STAR BRIGHT,
                    LET ALL TROUBLES CEASE,
                    GIVE ME THE WISH I WISH TO-NIGHT,
                    MAY ALL THE CHILDREN OF THIS WORLD
                    SLEEP IN PEACE.

*She goes back to sleep and almost immediately PETER flies into the room followed by TINK.*

PETER:        Tink, quick! Close the window. *(The window slams shut)* Make sure the catch is on. Now when Wendy comes back she will think her mother has locked her out and she will come back to me.

*TINK rumbles a few sulking notes.*

PETER:        But who's this? It's Wendy's mother. She's quite a pretty lady but not as pretty as my mother.

MRS DARL:    Wendy...

PETER:        There are two wet things sitting on her eyes. Now there are two more.

MRS DARL:    Wendy Wendy Wendy...

PETER: She is awfully fond of Wendy but I am fond of her too. We can't both have her, lady.

*MRS DARLING stirs in her sleep.*

PETER: She wants me to open the window. Well I won't!

*TINK pleads hopefully.*

PETER: Oh, all right then. Who wants silly mothers anyway? Come on, Tink.

*The window opens and PETER and TINK fly out just as WENDY, JOHN and MICHAEL quietly enter and regard the sleeping MRS DARLING.*

WENDY: Look, the window is open. You see? Peter was wrong.

MICHAEL: Is that our mother?

WENDY: Yes, yes.

MICHAEL: I think I've been here before.

JOHN: It's your home, stupid.

WENDY: There's your old bed, look.

JOHN: I say, the kennel! *(He peers inside)* There's a man sleeping in it. It's father!

MICHAEL: Can I see father? *(He looks)* Yes, that's father all right.

JOHN: I don't remember father sleeping in a kennel.

WENDY: Maybe we don't remember the old life as well as we thought we did. Shhh!

*MRS DARLING has stirred. And now she wakes, gets up, and walks to the window, taking in the CHILDREN as she passes them.*

| | |
|---|---|
| MRS DARL: | I see them so often in my dreams that I seem still to see them when I am awake. I'll not look again. *(So she looks out of the window)* So often their silver voices call me, my little children whom I'll never see again. |
| WENDY: | Mother. |
| MRS DARL: | That is Wendy. |
| JOHN: | Mother? |
| MRS DARL: | John. |
| MICHAEL: | *(A squeak)* Mother! |
| MRS DARL: | And Michael. And when they call I stretch out my arms to them. *(She turns and does so)*. But they never come. |

*Only this time they do in a concerted rush. Ad libs of "mummy, mother, oh my children, my darlings, you're home" etc. Then*

| | |
|---|---|
| MR DARL: | *(As he crawls out of the kennel)* A little less noise there if you please. |
| MRS DARL: | George! It's the children! They're home! Look, children, Nana's put your night things out for you. She has done that every evening since you went away. Poor Nana. She's pined so for you. |
| MR DARL: | Poor Nana. What about poor father? |
| JOHN: | Why have you been sleeping in Nana's kennel, father? |
| MRS DARL: | Out of remorse, my dear. But now that you are back all can be forgiven and things can be exactly as they were. |
| WENDY: | Well, not exactly as they were, mother. You see... |
| MRS DARL: | Yes? |

*WENDY turns to JOHN and MICHAEL. How does she start to explain? But all they do is shrug their shoulders. WENDY doesn't have to explain however for at that moment*

BOYS(Off): A HOUSE HAS A FLOOR...

*And they troop in followed by LISA.*

> AND A NEAT FRONT DOOR,
> FOUR WALLS OR MORE,
> AND A WATERPROOF ROOF.
>
> A HOUSE WILL HAVE BEDS,
> WITH COMF'TABLE SPREADS,
> TO LAY YOUR HEADS,
> AT THE END OF THE DAY.
>
> BUT A HOUSE IS NOT A HOME WITHOUT A MOTHER,
> A HOUSE IS NOT A HOME WITHOUT A MUM,
> MORE THAN A SISTER OR A BROTHER,
> SHE'LL ALWAYS BE A BOY'S BEST CHUM.

MRS DARL: Who...what...?

WENDY: These are the lost boys, mother. This is Tootles, and Slightly, Curly, Nibs, the twins. Will you adopt them? Can they stay?

*SMEE appears at the door with NANA.*

MRS DARL: And this?

JOHN: Oh, this is lovable old Smee. He needs a mother too.

NANA: Woof woof.

GEORGE: Lost boys, hey?

SMEE: And a lost pirate. Pardon, ex-pirate.

MR DARL: Pirate! By jellyfish and barnacles now that is interesting.

MRS DARL: George! What are we going to do?

MR DARL: Do? Why feed them of course. Come on everybody, down to the mess deck. Lisa, food, girl, food. We have a hungry crew on our hands.

*And, with cheers, yells, and a few "I complain ofs" there is a general dash for the door with only WENDY and MRS DARLING left behind.*

*PETER appears at the window.*

WENDY: Peter!

PETER: Hello, Wendy.

WENDY: Oh, I'm so glad you came.

MRS DARL: Peter?

WENDY: Oh, mother, *(grandly)* this... is Peter Pan.

MRS DARL: How do you do, Peter?

*PETER bows.*

WENDY: Peter, you don't feel you'd like to say anything to my parents? About a very sweet subject?

PETER: No, Wendy.

WENDY: About me, Peter.

PETER: No.

MRS DARL: Peter, let me adopt you too.

PETER: Would you send me to school?

MRS DARL: Yes.

PETER: And then to an office?

MRS DARL: Well, I suppose so.

PETER: Soon I would be grown-up?

MRS DARL: Yes.

PETER: No. I want always to be a little boy and have fun.

*He turns as if to fly away.*

WENDY: Mother, may I go with him?

MRS DARL: Certainly not. I have got you home again and I mean to keep you.

WENDY: But he does so need a mother.

MRS DARL: So do you, my love.

WENDY: Oh, all right.

MRS DARL: But, Peter, I shall let her go to you once a year for a week to do your spring cleaning.

WENDY: Oh, yes, yes!

MRS DARL: So I'll leave you to say your good-byes, Wendy. I'd better see what the pirates are up to downstairs. You know what your father is like. Good-night, Peter.

*And she goes. PETER flies further into the room.*

WENDY: Peter, you won't forget me, will you, before spring cleaning time comes?

PETER: Of course not.

WENDY: Then it's good-bye.

PETER: Yes.

WENDY: Peter! If another little girl, if one younger than I am... Oh, Peter, how I wish I could take you up and squidge you.

*PETER flies for the window.*

WENDY: Yes, I know. No one can ever touch you. Isn't that sad?

PETER: No! *(Pointing and with a note of triumph)* Never Land. Second to the right and straight on till morning!

*And he has gone. WENDY runs to the window.*

WENDY: Second to the right and straight on till morning.

ALL MY LIFE, I KNOW I WILL SPEND
EACH WAKING MOMENT WOND'RING
WHERE YOU ARE, HOW COULD YOU LEAVE ME THIS WAY?
THOUGH THE YEARS WILL FLY
THE MEMORIES WILL ALWAYS STAY.

SAY YOU'LL REMEMBER ME YOUR WHOLE LIFE THROUGH,
I WILL KNOW THE REASON I BELIEVE IN YOU,
I'LL HAVE THE MEMORIES YOU LEFT BEHIND,
FOREVER IS A LONG LONG TIME.
YOU'VE TAKEN MY HEART, AND NOW YOU WILL TEAR IT APART,
CHASING SHADOWS IN THE DARK,
YOU GAVE ME YOUR KISS, AND HOW I'M GOING TO MISS YOU.

SAY YOU'LL REMEMBER ME YOUR WHOLE LIFE THROUGH,
I WILL KNOW THE REASON I BELIEVE IN YOU,
WE'LL HAVE THE MEMORIES WE LEFT BEHIND,
FOREVER IS A LONG LONG TIME,

JUST SAY YOUR LOVE FOR ME WILL NEVER DIE,
FOREVER IS A LONG LONG TIME.

*She sits on the window seat gazing at the stars and that is where we leave her as the MUSIC SWELLS and the CURTAIN comes down.*

CURTAIN CALLS

a)                 ORCHESTRAL

b)                 I THINK WE KNEW IT WOULDN'T LAST,
WHY DID IT HAVE TO GO SO FAST?
WE WERE HAVING A REALLY GOOD TIME TOGETHER.
WE'VE BEEN THE BEST OF FRIENDS,
I HATE TO SEE US BREAK UP,
BUT ALL GOOD THINGS MUST HAVE AN END,
I GUESS IT'S TIME TO WAKE UP.

READY TO GO, FACING THE DAY,
TIME DOESN'T WAIT, LIFE'S NOT ALL PLAY,
BUT WE DID HAVE A WONDERFUL TIME,
YES WE DID HAVE A WONDERFUL TIME,
A GLORIOUS, FABULOUS, WONDERFUL,
UNFORGETTABLE TIME,
TOGETHER.

c)                 NOBODY NEEDS TO BE TOLD, (WOOF WOOF)
A DOG AS NURSEMAID,
DISPENSING THE FIRST AID'S
A PET WITH A HEART OF GOLD.

WHAT IF HER NOSE MAY BE COLD (WOOF WOOF)
AND OFTEN QUITE RUNNY?
SHE'S WARM AND SHE'S FUNNY,
THIS DOG WITH A HEART OF GOLD. (WOOF WOOF, WOOF WOOF)

SHE'S BRAVE SHE'S CUTE,

SHE'S MOST ASTUTE,
SHE HAS THE GENTLEST OF JAWS.
AND IF YOU'RE CHRONIC AND NEED A TONIC,
YOU'RE IN THE SAFEST OF PAWS. (WOOF WOOF)

A TREASURE NOT TO BE SOLD, (WOOF WOOF)
SHE'S ONE IN A MILLION,
YES, SOME SAY A TRILLION,
THIS DOG WITH A HEART OF GOLD (WOOF WOOF)

AND I WISH SHE WERE MY MOTHER.
THIS DOG WITH A HEART OF GOLD.

The End

# Props List

## Act One

### Scene 1

3 Night Lights
Jar on Mantelpiece
Clothes brush on chest of drawers
Books on bedside cabinets
2 medicine bottles
2 spoons
Medicine glasses
Nana's bowl
Chocolates
Shadow
Soap
Sewing kit with needle/ thread/ thimble
Acorn button on Peter's jerkin
Dagger in sheath – Peter
Umbrella – John
Book
Doll or teddy bear

### Scene 3

Musical pipes – Slightly
Bow/ arrows – Tootles
Treasure chest with gold chocolates
Cutlasses
Daggers
Pistols
Muskets
Bosun's whistle
Lace handkerchief – Hook
Grubby handkerchief – Smee
Tomahawks
Trick arrow – Wendy
Acorn on chain – Wendy
Special shoe for knocker – Tootles
Special top hat for chimney - John

Scene 4
Palanquin

Scene 5
Ornamental comb – Mermaid
Rowboat/ oars/ ropes


# Act Two

Scene 2
Bedding/ pillows
Basket bed
Board table on tree trunk
Toadstools
Musical pipes – Peter
Seashells – Peter's medicine
Poison bottle – Hook

Scene 3
Rope/ bonds

Scene 4
Barrels
Sewing machine
Material
Telescope
Ropes
Plank
Lantern (practical)

Furniture - Nursery

3 beds
3 bedside cabinets
Chest of drawers
Small table
Towel rail
Kennel
Chair

Other Titles Available

## PLAYS

ARE YOU SITTING COMFORTABLY
AU PAIR
BEAUTIFUL FOR EVER
BETWEEN TWO SIGHS
EARLY ONE MORNING
GENERATIONS
HEAR THE HYENA LAUGH
HOW DO YOU LIKE YOUR WAGNER
LITTLE FOOTSTEPS ON THE PETALS
OH BROTHER!
RED IN THE MORNING
ROSEMARY
THE 88
THIRD DRAWER FROM THE TOP
THRILLER OF THE YEAR
TWILIGHT OF AUNT EDNA
WOMEN AROUND

## MUSICALS

BLACK MARIA
CHAMPAGNE CHARLIE
CUPID
FUGUE IN TWO FLATS
LA BELLE OTERO


For information on this
or any other available plays please contact:

info@dcgmediagroup.com    www.dcgmediagroup.com

www.ingramcontent.com/pod-product-compliance
Lightning Source LLC
Chambersburg PA
CBHW020015050426
42450CB00005B/488